WHAT FISH?

A BUYER'S GUIDE TO REEF FISH

PHIL HUNT

BARRON'S

First edition for the United States
and Canada published in 2009 by
Barron's Educational Series, Inc.

First published in 2009 by
Interpet Publishing.
© Copyright 2009 by Interpet
Publishing.

All inquiries should be addressed to:
Barron's Educational Series, Inc.
250 Wireless Boulevard
Hauppauge, New York 11788
www.barronseduc.com

ISBN-13: 978-0-7641-4306-9
ISBN-10: 0-7641-4306-9

Library of Congress Control
  Number: 2009920837

Printed in China
9 8 7 6 5 4 3 2 1

The star rating ★★★★★

We include a guide to the prices that aquarists might expect to
pay for individuals of each species. The range of prices for each
group of reef fishes is given on the opening page of the section.
Sometimes, the star rating for a particular fish or group of fishes
will cover more than one price category. Prices may vary from
shop to shop, and in some cases even according to the season:
Most marine fishes are wild-caught and in some areas certain
species are more readily available at some times than others.

Author

Growing up in South
Yorkshire in the late
1960s, Phil Hunt became
interested in aquariums
when he started school and found a tropical
community tank there. Having pestered his parents successfully for
a tank of his own, he then kept freshwater tropicals for several years.
After a break of a few years, while he acquired a degree from the
University of Leeds and a doctorate from the University of York (neither
of which is related to fish), he started keeping reef aquariums in the
early 1990s. Since then he has been a
regular contributor to fishkeeping
magazines, most notably
Practical Fishkeeping. He
has also written *The Reef
Aquarium* for Interpet
Publishing. Phil lives
in Sussex with his
wife, daughter, son,
and quite a lot of
marine life.

Contents

In this listing, the common name is followed by its scientific name.

▲ *The maroon clownfish (Premnas biaculeatus), is aggressive with other fishes, but safe with corals.*

Introduction

A well-designed, well-maintained reef tank is perhaps the most beautiful of all aquariums. Corals and other invertebrates, with their fascinating and often bizarre forms and astonishing colors, together with the intricate background provided by living rock, create beautiful underwater landscapes, virtually unparalleled in other types of aquarium. The reef aquarium is fast becoming the standard marine tank, as technology and techniques have improved to the point where what was once the province of dedicated enthusiasts has now become accessible to most fishkeepers. As a result, in recent years there has been a distinct shift away from the more traditional fish-only marine aquarium.

With this change in the type of marine aquarium that most people keep, there has been a corresponding shift in the types of fishes that live in them. Initially, reef aquarium keepers were very conservative in both the types of fishes they kept, and how many. In the early days of reef aquariums, keeping most invertebrates was difficult, and any fishes that were kept had to pose absolutely no threat to corals. Also, early reef aquariums struggled to maintain water quality adequate for coral growth. As a result, reef aquarium keepers tried to minimize the load on the system—by keeping very few, usually small, fishes.

Since then, the development of aquarium systems based on live rock and other "living" substrates has revolutionized biological filtration, and fish stocking levels are no longer an issue. Developments in lighting and techniques of maintaining calcium and alkalinity levels have made it possible to keep invertebrates that were once the stuff of dreams. Reefkeepers have also been able to widen the range of fishes they keep, discovering that fishes are not only attractive and interesting, but can also be useful. Not all the fish that can be kept in reef aquariums would be suitable for every such tank—in some cases only a narrow selection of corals can be kept with a particular fish species—but this expanded range of fishes does open up new possibilities for reefkeepers.

▼ *Springer's dottyback from the Red Sea is one of the smallest of its family, and a great fish for the nano-reef aquarium.*

Contents

▼ *The harlequin tuskfish*
(Choerodon fasciatus) *is a robust and colorful wrasse suitable for a large reef aquarium.*

92–115
Tangs and surgeonfishes

116–131
Gobies

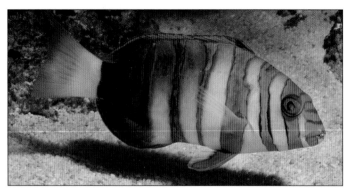

▲ *The appealing yellow coral goby (Gobiodon okinawae) is a tiny fish, ideal for the nano-reef aquarium.*

Contents

▲ *The majestic angel (Pomacanthus navarchus) is a stunning fish and suitable for some reef aquariums.*

▼ *The spectacular niger trigger*
(Odonus niger) *can reach 18 in.
(45 cm) and needs a very large tank
with generous swimming space.*

Part One
Getting Started

▶ No reef aquarium could possibly accommodate every one of the species described in this book. In this section we therefore provide advice on refining the selection of species for the aquarium. We describe how to minimize the territorial aggression of many reef fishes in order to assemble harmonious communities; provide guidance on how to decide how many fishes to keep in a given tank and how large those fishes should be; how to combine fishes with invertebrates safely, and how to select healthy individual fishes. Also, as not every reef aquarium suits every type of fish, we describe how to tailor the aquarium to meet the needs of specific fishes. Finally, we examine how best to deal with any health problems that may occasionally arise.

▶ *Selecting the right fishes is the key to success.*

Choosing fish species

▶ When choosing a selection of fishes to keep in the reef aquarium, the process usually starts by considering the needs of the other inhabitants of the tank. Traditionally, this has meant considering only fishes that are compatible with a wide range of invertebrates, including shrimps, hermit crabs, snails, and starfishes of various kinds, as well as corals, anemones, and clams. This obviously narrows the range of fishes that can be kept quite considerably, but still leaves a good selection of attractive and interesting species; the majority of the fishes described in this book fall into this category.

Traditionally, judgments about "reef safety" were made at a family level: Gobies would be considered safe, triggerfishes would not. More recently, as experience with reef aquariums and knowledge about marine fishes has grown, it has become clear that there are quite a few more species that fit into the traditional "reef-safe" category. These include members

The pivotal fish approach

A fish is the key inhabitant and the other members of the community are chosen to suit it.

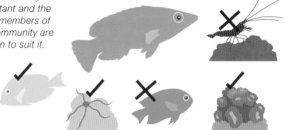

of some families that were previously considered unsuitable—triggerfishes and butterflyfishes, for example. However, some members of apparently safe families have proved to be less innocuous than they were thought to be; examples include some blennies.

Just as significantly, it has proven possible to keep a much wider variety of fishes in the reef aquarium if the range of invertebrates is restricted to some degree. For example, many fishes eat shrimps, but are perfectly safe with sessile invertebrates. Other fishes may pick at some species of corals but not others. The gradual increase in knowledge and experience with different fishes in different reef tank settings has greatly expanded the possibilities with respect to fishes that can be kept in this type of aquarium.

Building fish communities in the reef aquarium—thinking ahead

There are several good approaches to assembling a community of fishes for a reef aquarium. The

thing that unites them is that they involve planning and forethought. Of course, it is possible simply to set up an aquarium and then look for some fishes to put in it. However, this is not a great approach, as there is a risk of discovering that a highly desirable fish is not a good fit with the existing aquarium, and either having to forgo the fish or redesign the tank. Here are some better strategies:

The pivotal fish approach

Here, a particular fish is the main attraction and the aquarium is created around it, providing an appropriate physical environment and tankmates (see pages 194–203). An example would be an aquarium designed around the lovely Helfrich's firefish (*Nemateleotris helfrichi*). This deep-water species appreciates relatively subdued lighting, which limits the selection of corals that can be kept with it (bubble corals, *Plerogyra* species, *Trachyphyllia* brain corals, and mushroom anemones would

***Above:** Tangs make great inhabitants for a variety of reef aquariums. This kole and yellow tang were added at the same time.*

The pivotal invertebrate approach

*Other tank inhabitants
are selected to
be compatible with
a chosen invertebrate.*

geographical area and/or reef zone are the starting point. An example might be a large Red Sea biotope aquarium featuring a sailfin tang (*Zebrasoma desjardinii*), a purple tang (*Z. xanthurum),* and various dottybacks endemic to the region, such as *Pseudochromis fridmani, P. sankeyi,* and *P. springeri*, with the aquarium laid out to suit these species (dense rock structures for the dottybacks, open water for the tangs).

be ideal). As a habitat, it needs plenty of rocks and caves into which it can dart when frightened. It is quite a shy fish, and other fish kept with it need to be of similar temperament—ideal choices might be various dartfishes (*Ptereleotris* species).

The pivotal invertebrate approach

Here, a specific type of invertebrate is the focus of the aquarium, so the chosen fishes will be compatible with those invertebrates and will live in the type of habitat that the invertebrates require. An example would be an aquarium focused on the larger *Tridacna* species clams. They need intense lighting and a fairly large tank to accommodate their growth. The selection of fishes is restricted to some degree. Deep-water species that do not appreciate bright light will not be suitable. You must also exclude any marginally reef-safe species that may try to eat the clams' mantles or their mucus, such as angelfishes (except *Genicanthus* species) and

algae-eating blennies. However, some fishes could be beneficial for the clams: *Zebrasoma* tangs can keep shells clear of filamentous algae, and pyjama wrasses (*Pseudocheilinus hexataenia*) and similar species can keep parasitic snails under control. You can then choose other fishes that would not harm the clams and would get along with these species.

The biotope approach

In this case, fishes and/or invertebrates from a particular

The biotope approach

*Creatures from a specific
habitat in a particular area
are kept together.*

The reef garden approach

Similar to the way that many freshwater planted tanks are designed, the aquarium inhabitants are selected primarily to create an attractive underwater scene—but all the inhabitants need to be compatible and suitable for the aquarium environment. This approach involves the most detailed planning, but the result can be spectacular. An example might be a large tank with strong surging currents and intense lighting, mainly stocked with *Acropora* corals of a variety

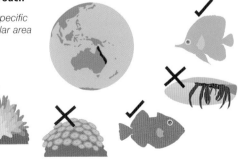

The reef garden approach

Fishes and invertebrates that are compatible and look good together are selected mainly for appearance.

of colors and forms. To bring movement to this spectacular reefscape, add a shoal of nine Bartlett's anthias *(Pseudanthias bartlettorum)*, which are ideally suited to this type of environment as well as highly attractive when kept as a group. Also add a kole tang *(Ctenochaetus strigosus)* and a sailfin tang *(Zebrasoma veliferum)*. The latter are both

adapted to live in the brightly lit, turbulent water of the upper reef slope, contrast in color, shape, and size to the anthias, and provide a useful service in eating nuisance algae.

Selecting individual fishes
However carefully the fish community is designed, problems will result if unhealthy fishes are

added to the aquarium. Choosing healthy fishes can make a great contribution to the success of the reef aquarium. The first choice to make is the right aquarium dealer; good dealers select their livestock with care and thus make life simpler for their customers.

When presented with a selection of fishes in a dealer's tanks, there are several key things to check in order to pick out a healthy individual:

• Healthy fishes are alert, active, and interested in what is happening around them, but the mix of species in a dealer's tank may affect the appearance of a fish in this respect. A more aggressive tankmate may lead to a perfectly healthy fish being rather reclusive—but this situation should be fairly obvious.

• Body conformation is a good indicator of health. A healthy fish

Left: Carefully selecting individual fishes can minimize problems. There are various indicators of good health that fishkeepers can use as a guide.

should look sleek and plump, with a well-rounded belly and no "pinched" areas (particularly on the back, behind the head).

• The eyes should be clear and bright, and the fins intact with no bloody streaks, cloudy areas, or frayed edges. However, minor damage is not usually significant. The mouth should look perfect, as in some species, damage to the mouthparts may doom the fish to starve.

• Colors should be bright, but note that many species can change the intensity of their colors according to lighting, background, and mood. Also, the use of low levels of copper (for disease prevention) in dealers' tanks may make fish look less colorful—a situation that usually resolves on introduction to copper-free water.

• Apparently endless hunger is a good sign in most species, and asking to see a fish feeding before

Above: Healthy fishes always seem hungry—seeing them feed is a great indicator of good condition.

buying it is a time-honored way of checking the health of a new specimen.

• Fishes should show no obvious signs of disease such as skin lesions, rapid breathing, hanging listlessly in water currents, or scratching against rocks or tank fittings.

Tailoring the aquarium

▶ The coral reef provides a wide range of different environments, and the fishes that are kept in the aquarium come from a variety of habitats. Some fishes live among coral heads, others in open water, still others on sandy or muddy seabeds, and others in caves. Some species roam over reef crests in highly turbulent water; others live in calm lagoons. Different species are found at depths ranging from a few inches beneath the surface to more than 24 in. (60 cm) down.

Faced with fishes from such a variety of natural habitats, it is clear that a "standard" reef aquarium— however that is defined—cannot provide an ideal environment for every species: a "one size fits all" approach does not work. A number of factors can be manipulated to tailor the reef aquarium to suit particular species of fishes. These include the following:

• The light intensity
• The water currents
• The tank substrate (the type and depth of sand or gravel used)
• The underwater landscape
• The types of invertebrates that are present

With some of these factors, it is possible to accommodate several variations within a single tank. For example, it is possible to include several different types of base substrate in a single aquarium, or (especially in large tanks) to construct an underwater landscape that includes both dense aggregations of live rock and corals

and expanses of open water. Water movement and light intensity are more difficult, but not impossible, to vary within a single aquarium.

An important point when considering all of these factors is that they really need to be addressed when the aquarium is being planned. This means thinking carefully, before the aquarium is set up, about which fishes will be kept and then setting up the tank in a way that will suit these species. This approach will pay off in the long term, allowing the development of a settled, healthy community of fishes that will behave as naturally as possible.

Light intensity
Underwater light intensity is largely determined by depth, and fishes that are collected in deeper water can sometimes find it difficult to

Above: *Intense lighting is a feature of many reef aquariums, but it does not suit all fishes. These LED systems are bright and durable.*

adapt to the very intense lighting that is a feature of many reef aquariums. Examples of such fishes include some *Genicanthus* angelfishes, some of the fairy wrasses (*Cirrhilabrus* species), and some species of *Pseudanthias* wreckfishes.

Another group of fishes that prefer relatively subdued lighting in the aquarium are those that in the wild prefer to live in caves or under overhangs. These include fishes such as forktails (*Assessor* species), some cardinalfishes, and grammas. In some cases these are fishes that tend to be most active at twilight, and spend the day in caves before emerging onto the

not like the full glare of intense lighting. This approach works particularly well with those species that like to lurk among overhanging rocks. Providing dimly lit areas can also help deep-water fishes to acclimatize to bright conditions by giving them places to retreat when necessary. Large plating or mushroom-shaped corals can also be used to provide shade.

Water currents

The degree and type of water movement in the aquarium is of great importance to corals, but it may come as a surprise that it is also significant to fishes. Different parts of the reef have different patterns of water movement, and fishes that live in specific zones are

reef as the evening comes, but they also include species that are adapted to life with a roof over their heads, as it were.

Most of the fishes in these categories will eventually become accustomed to the very bright conditions in an aquarium devoted to *Acropora* stony corals and tridacnid clams, but this can be a slow process, during which the fish may be stressed and reluctant to feed. It is far better to provide them with something closer to the light intensity they would expect in the wild.

In a reef aquarium, however, the type of lighting in use generally reflects the requirements of the invertebrate inhabitants, namely corals and clams. This means

Above: Live rock is a key part of the aquarium environment, providing hiding and resting places for fishes such as this wrasse.

that it is difficult to adjust the light intensity to suit particular fishes, so either the fishes must be chosen to suit the existing lighting regimen, or the fishes and invertebrates must be chosen at the aquarium design stage (which is always good practice) and the lighting arranged to suit them.

One other option is to create bright and dark zones within the aquarium when aquascaping the tank. Live rock can be used to construct large caves and, with care, overhangs that can provide shady zones for fishes that do

Above: Powerful water currents suit many reef fishes as well as corals. Propeller pumps can provide movement at the surface.

Above: *A mix of rocky areas, open water, and large invertebrates suits the clownfish and yellow tang in this aquarium very well.*

adapted to the currents in these areas. Fishes that range over the reef crest, for example, are adapted to powerful surging currents, and the high dissolved oxygen levels associated with such areas. Examples of such fishes include surgeonfishes, such as the Achilles tang *(Acanthurus achilles)* and the powder blue tang *(A. leucosternon).* Strong water movement and high oxygen levels are essential for success with these species.

At the other end of the spectrum are fishes from very calm waters; these may be unable to swim against very strong currents or may find it difficult to capture planktonic prey when this is being swept by at high speed. Classic examples of such fishes are sea horses.

As with lighting, the water movement in the reef aquarium is usually set up to suit particular invertebrates, and so either the fish and invertebrates need to be chosen together when the aquarium is being planned, or fishes need to be selected that will fit in with the available conditions.

Substrates

Sand, mud, and gravel play an important role in the lives of many aquarium fishes. The substrate can be a source of food, a place to build a burrow, or somewhere to hide or to sleep, among other things. In the aquarium, there are three key aspects of the substrate that can be adapted to suit particular fishes: the particle size, the extent or area of the bed, and its depth.

The particle size of the material used—how fine the sand or gravel is—is important to fishes for several reasons. Species that feed by sifting sand, taking it in through the mouth, and either spitting it out or passing it through the gills after extracting anything edible,

need fine sands. Several species of gobies feed in this way. Very fine sands are also best for fishes that dive into the sand either to hide when frightened or to sleep. These include many wrasses (see pages 70–91) and tilefishes (see pages 156–159). Such fishes often dive into the sand at great speed and can suffer injuries (typically to the snout) if they attempt to bury themselves in coarser material.

However, coarse gravel is preferred by those species that build burrows, as it makes construction easier. Typical burrow

builders are jawfishes and gobies, in the latter case particularly those that live in symbiotic relationships with pistol shrimps—although in these combinations it is the shrimps that do the hard work.

The area of sand bed available is principally of importance to those species that tend to hide in the sand when disturbed—tilefishes and some wrasses, for example, and to sand-sifting gobies. For these species it is best to provide a large open area of sand bed.

The depth of the sand is important for several reasons.

How fishes use sand and gravel beds

Blue-cheeked gobies feed by sifting mouthfuls of fine sand to find small worms and crustaceans.

Fine sand

Above: *Shrimp gobies, such as this* Amblyeleotris *species, like coarse sand and gravel to help them build burrows.*

Many fishes live in burrows and can build these most easily in coarse sand and gravel.

Banana wrasses dive into soft sand beds when frightened and to sleep.

Coarse gravel

Burrowing fishes, with or without pistol shrimp partners, prefer deep beds to accommodate their burrows. For fishes that sleep in the substrate, a deep bed of fine sand is best, and the larger the fish, the deeper the sand needs to be.

Fortunately, it is not difficult to have a mixture of different substrate types in the aquarium, especially in a large tank. Areas of both fine sand and coarser material can be provided, and the bed can be made deeper in some areas than others. For those fishes, particularly tilefishes, that need large expanses of open sand bed this needs to be a major feature of the aquarium landscape.

Aquascapes
In addition to the choice of substrate, there are other decisions to make with respect to the physical layout of the aquarium.

Above: Dottybacks, such as this Pseudochromis flavivertex, do best in aquariums with plenty of hiding places. Empty shells are ideal.

A coral reef offers a tremendous variety of different habitats for fishes, and this is one reason for the huge diversity of species found in this environment. As a result, coral reef fishes tend to have distinct preferences in terms of their physical environment. Fortunately, the layout of the aquarium can be easily adapted to suit the needs of different fishes. The key issue is to find the right balance between open water and solid structures (rocks and invertebrates). Although most reef aquarium fishes require some form of shelter into which to retreat when sleeping or frightened, some species spend most of their time close to hard substrates, either grazing algal films (Centropyge angelfishes, see pages 172–178) or hunting small invertebrates (Pseudochromis dottybacks, see pages 66–68). For such species it would be almost impossible to have too much rock in the aquarium. Paradoxically, the more rock or other cover there is, the more you will see such fishes, as the constant proximity of somewhere to hide gives them confidence to stay out on view.

Other types of fishes, particularly planktivorous species, require much more open swimming space. Such fishes are often fast swimmers, chasing their food in open water. A tank with too much rock and too many corals will not provide them with the space they need. Such fishes would often be well served by a tank with just enough cover to provide them with somewhere to sleep.

Between these extremes lie many other fishes that appreciate plenty of open water, but require

hard substrates either for grazing (tangs and large angels, for example) or hunting small invertebrates (basses, for instance). At the extreme end of the latter category are some species that require a sufficient quantity of live rock to supply them with small creatures to eat, as they tend not to accept prepared foods. Mandarins and scooters are the most commonly kept of such species.

As well as these quite general habitat preferences, there are, of course, species with much more specific needs: As one simple example, cave dwellers should be provided with caves.

In practice, it is often straightforward in large aquariums to accommodate a wide variety of different habitat needs. Areas of densely packed rocks and invertebrates can be interspersed with open areas of sand; caves can be created, but plenty of swimming space preserved. In smaller tanks, it is necessary to decide what kinds of fishes to keep, and then create the type of habitat that will suit them—or vice versa.

Invertebrate companions
Invertebrates are, of course, a key element of the reef aquarium, and have an influence on which fishes are best suited to a particular tank. Unlike the other aspects of the reef aquarium environment, however, the concern is not so much for the fishes as for the invertebrates— although there are exceptions. Most of the fishes described in this book are safe to keep with any sessile invertebrates, but for those species that are on the fringes of being suitable for reef aquariums,

Above: Feathery polyps, such as Anthelia, Clavularia, and Xenia, may be eaten by grazing fishes. Choose tank inhabitants with care.

the choice of corals can be critical. These species include angelfishes, both the *Centropyge* pygmy angels and larger species (but not the planktivorous *Genicanthus* species, which are usually safe with all corals), butterflyfishes, rabbitfishes, triggers, and even herbivorous blennies. All of these fishes may have some inclination to eat or at least sample sessile invertebrates. Fortunately, not all invertebrates are particularly palatable, even to grazing fishes. Some are far more likely to be the targets of unwelcome attention than others. The most likely sessile invertebrates to be eaten or sampled by these borderline reef aquarium fishes are low-growing feathery polyps such as star polyps (*Pachyclavularia* species and their

relatives), fleshy stony corals with large polyps but without potent stings (exemplified by *Trachyphyllia* brain corals, but also including *Lobophyllia, Scolymia,* and *Cynarina* species, among others), and tridacnid clams. Almost any fish that has any tendency at all to consume invertebrates, or at least try them, is likely to sample these species. *Pachyclavularia* and

similar species are sometimes even eaten by tangs, which are usually excellent reef aquarium fishes.

At the opposite end of the spectrum are a range of corals that are seldom bothered by most fishes (although some coral-grazing butterflyfishes would probably eat them). These include mushroom anemones, and leather corals and their relatives, such as *Sinularia* species. Some of these species are known to contain toxic chemicals (presumably to discourage predation), and it may be that these make them taste unpleasant to fishes. These corals are generally the best choices for reef aquariums with fishes such as large angels.

Most of the commonly kept corals fall between these extremes, but there are some trends in vulnerability. Small-polyp stony corals, such as *Acropora* and *Montipora* species, are often left alone by many fishes, where corals with larger polyps would be

Below: Mushroom anemones, available in various color morphs, are seldom damaged by fishes, which find them unpalatable.

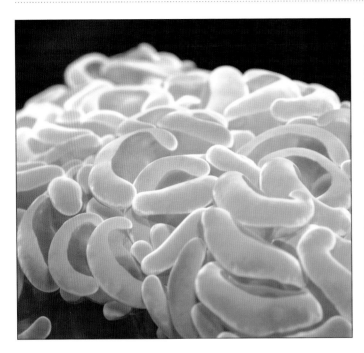

Euphyllia species) can catch and eat small or slow-moving fishes such as neon gobies and their relatives (*Elacatinus* species) and mandarins and scooters (*Synchiropus* species). These types of fishes are also at risk from some large mushroom anemones, which will enclose and trap them. These predatory corals should be kept only with larger and/or more active fishes. This is

Below: *Boxing shrimps are less likely to be eaten than their smaller relatives, but may predate on small, slow-moving fishes.*

damaged or eaten. Large-polyp corals with strong stings (such as *Euphyllia* species) are somewhat less likely to be predated on than their more innocuous cousins, but their stings do not offer absolute protection; they will still be eaten by some butterflyfishes, for example.

Careful selection of corals means that reef aquariums can be created that house some surprising fishes: Some butterflyfishes that eat stony corals can be kept with certain soft coral species, for example. This type of approach can be used to widen considerably the range of fishes that can be kept in a reef aquarium, even if the tank houses only a restricted

Above: *This* Euphyllia *has potent stings to ward off the attentions of most fishes, but is still at risk from butterflyfishes, among others.*

range of corals. Mixing fishes and invertebrates in this way is at a relatively new and experimental stage, however, and fishkeepers should proceed with caution, not risking any valued corals with potential predators.

Finally, in some cases the selection of invertebrates in the tank can have a deleterious effect on fishes rather than vice versa. Corals with powerful stings (typical examples would be bubble corals, *Plerogyra* species, elegance corals, *Catalaphyllia jardinei*, and particularly the case for very large mushroom anemones ("elephant ear" mushrooms, *Amplexidiscus fenestrafer*) that grow up to 18 in. (45 cm) across and are notorious predators of even quite substantial fishes—including, remarkably, clownfishes, which are not usually at risk from corals.

A few other invertebrates pose a risk to fishes. The large green brittlestar *Ophiarachna incrassata* is an infamous fish eater, and large boxing shrimps and their relatives (*Stenopus* species) also sometimes catch and eat small fishes.

Above: *Many soft corals contain toxins that make them unappetizing to fishes.*

Dealing with problems

▶ Like all plants and animals, fishes are susceptible to a range of diseases. In a well-managed reef aquarium with carefully chosen fishes, disease problems are likely to be very rare, but it is important to know how to prevent them and to recognize and treat them if they should occur.

The diseases most commonly seen in the reef aquarium are head and lateral line erosion (HLLE) and white spot disease (*Cryptocaryon irritans* infection, sometimes also called marine ich). Other problems occasionally seen are velvet disease (*Amyloodinium ocellatum* infection); brooklynella (*Brooklynella hostilis* infection); *Uronema* infections; swimbladder problems; external parasites; and gut parasites.

Head and lateral line erosion

This is also known as lateral line disease and is seen mainly in fishes that have a natural diet that includes a high proportion of algae, most commonly tangs and angelfishes. It manifests as loss of skin and, in severe cases, erosion of underlying tissue on the head and along the lateral line. The causes of HLLE are not completely understood: Viral infections, stray electrical currents in the tank water, and exposure to copper treatment have all been suggested. It appears much more likely to be related to a nutritional deficiency (probably of vitamin C and possibly vitamin A), although it Is possible that other factors may be involved. It can be prevented by feeding a diet rich in algae (for example, sheets or flakes

of dried seaweed). In mild cases at least, the disease can be reversed by such a diet.

White spot infection

This appears as small white spots on the skin or fins of an affected fish. Typically, it is first seen as just a few well-defined spots scattered over the body. These then disappear for a couple of days, but reappear in greater numbers. This process is repeated as the parasite goes through its life cycle, until the fish is densely covered in spots.

Below: This copperband butterfly is in the early stages of a white spot infection, as can be seen by the lesions in the tail fin.

Eventually, the gills are affected and/or secondary infections set in and, if untreated, the fish will probably die. White spot is highly infectious, so if an affected fish is not treated promptly, it is probable that its tankmates will soon be infected.

There are two reliable treatments for white spot: hyposalinity and copper (see panels). Ideally, both should be performed using a separate treatment tank (containing no live rock or invertebrates), although it is sometimes possible to use a mild form of hyposalinity treatment in the reef aquarium. Hyposalinity treatment is effective in most cases, and carries less risk than copper, but some cases

Full hyposalinity treatment procedure

(For use only in a separate treatment tank)

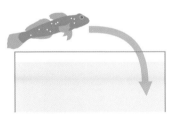

1 *Decrease the specific gravity of the tank water over several hours by removing salt water and adding fresh water. On the first day, take down specific gravity from the starting point (typically 1.025–1.027 to 1.017–1.018). Check the alkalinity and if necessary add a buffer to correct it.*

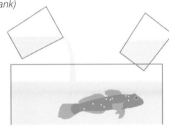

2 *Continue the process on day two, going from s.g. 1.017–1.018 to 1.010–1.012. Check the alkalinity again and adjust it if necessary.*

3 *The white spots should disappear quickly (usually in about three days). Keep the fish at this salinity for three weeks after the last lesions have gone. Check the alkalinity regularly and correct it as needed.*

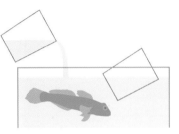

4 *Adjust the specific gravity back to normal over a period of two to three days by carrying out partial water changes with "extra-strength" seawater (water made up to s.g. of at least 1.030).*

5 *Observe the fish for one week to ensure that the infection does not return.*

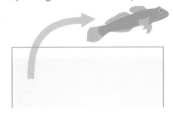

6 *Return the fish to the display aquarium.*

MILD HYPOSALINITY TREATMENT PROCEDURE

Many invertebrates will tolerate some reduction in salinity, provided it is done gradually. Notable exceptions are many echinoderms, particularly sea cucumbers and starfishes such as *Linckia* species (the commonly kept blue starfish *L. laevigata*, for example). It is best not to reduce salinity in tanks housing such species. Brittle stars and serpent stars are usually more tolerant.

Reducing the specific gravity (s.g.) from the normal 1.025–1.027 to around 1.018 is generally safe when done over three to four days and ensuring that the alkalinity remains at normal levels. This may be enough in some cases to clear the infection. Observe the affected fishes carefully, and if the spots disappear (if this is going to happen, it will occur within about five days), maintain the specific gravity at this level for around six weeks, before adjusting it back to normal over a period of three to four days.

In some cases it is possible to push the s.g. of the display tank lower, depending on what invertebrates are present. Leather corals and their relatives, star polyps, mushroom anemones, and the hardier stony corals, together with most hermit crabs and algae-eating snails, will all tolerate even lower salinities, down to s.g. 1.015, particularly if adjustments are made gradually. However, echinoderms and most shrimps may well be harmed, as may more sensitive corals.

(which seem to be caused by rare strains of *Cryptocaryon irritans* that are tolerant of low salinity) will respond only to copper.

If either form of mild hyposalinity fails to clear the infection, transfer the affected fish to a treatment tank and treat it with either full hyposalinity or copper.

Copper treatment

There are many copper-based treatments for white spot on the market. As copper is highly toxic to invertebrates, treatment must always be carried out in a separate aquarium rather than in a reef tank.

The best type of treatment to use is one based on non-chelated copper—these often contain copper sulphate. Add the treatment to the water in the treatment tank to a level recommended by the manufacturer. Use a test kit to measure the copper level, as getting the concentration exactly right is very important—overdosing can be fatal to fishes.

Treatment is typically continued for around 10 days (this may vary with different products, so be sure to follow the instructions). Check the copper level regularly. Adsorption of copper by aquarium

decor can cause the level to drop and require adjustment.

When treatment is finished, remove the copper by water changes and/or filtration with carbon. As with low-salinity treatment, observe the fish for a week or so after treatment to be sure there is no recurrence, then return it to the main tank (ensuring that no potentially copper-contaminated water is transferred with the fish).

Bear in mind that many species of fishes react badly to copper treatment. These are usually listed in the instructions provided with

Copper treatment for fish

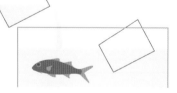

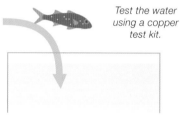

Test the water using a copper test kit.

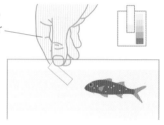

1 Add a copper treatment (ideally a non-chelated formulation) to the water in the treatment tank to a level recommended by the manufacturer.

2 Use a test kit to measure the copper level, as getting the concentration exactly right is very important. Transfer the affected fish to the treatment tank.

3 Continue the treatment for about 10 days (this may vary with different products, so be sure to follow the instructions), checking the copper level regularly.

4 When treatment is finished, remove the copper by water changes and/or filtration with carbon.

5 Observe the fish for a week or so after treatment to be sure there is no recurrence.

6 Return the fish to the main tank. Do not transfer any copper-contaminated water with the fish.

proprietary remedies. They include lionfishes, blennies, mandarins, and scooters, and some clownfish species (notably the Red Sea clownfish *Amphiprion bicinctus*), among others. Observe all fishes carefully during copper treatment, and if they show signs of distress, reduce the copper level rapidly, either by water changes or chemical filtration. Note that the colors of some species tend to fade during copper treatment; if the fish otherwise behaves normally, this is not a cause for concern and the color should return when the fish is back in its usual environment.

Velvet disease
Fortunately, velvet disease is much less common than white spot. It is a much more virulent infection than white spot and requires more rapid treatment. It is caused by a dinoflagellate parasite called *Amyloodinium ocellatum*. It is more difficult to diagnose than white

spot—the characteristic sprinkling of very fine spots on the skin giving the "velvety" appearance described in textbooks often occurs only late in the infection. Earlier signs include rapid breathing, scratching on rocks, lying inactive on the bottom of the tank (in a species that is usually active), and a loss of appetite—particularly if this is in combination with any of the other signs. Velvet disease should be treated with copper, following the manufacturer's instructions. This infection is rare in well-managed systems with sensibly chosen fishes, but it is highly infectious, so infected fishes should be removed from the aquarium and treated promptly.

Other infections
Very rarely, fishes may suffer from other parasitic infections, notably *Brooklynella hostilis* and *Uronema marinum*. *Brooklynella* infections most commonly affect wild-collected clownfishes (which

Above: Netting fishes in a well-stocked reef aquarium can be a nightmare, involving removing many of the rocks and invertebrates.

it is not advisable to keep, for this and other reasons). The infection manifests as overproduction of mucus, which appears as a whitish slimy film covering the body, coupled with rapid breathing and sometimes fading of colors. Treat it using a series of 15-minute freshwater dips.

Uronema infections tend to present with skin ulcers, excessive mucus production, rapid breathing, scratching on rocks, loss of color, and eventually weight loss. Hyposalinity treatment has been reported to be effective, as has treatment with methylene blue or malachite green.

Swimbladder problems
These cannot be treated, but it is worth knowing how to recognize

them, if only to be able to avoid buying affected fishes. These problems most frequently affect fishes collected in deep water, and seem to result from taking the fish up to the surface too quickly, without enough time for decompression.

Affected fishes typically seem unable to stay in position in the water, and may swim jerkily, sometimes with the body at an odd angle. They may even be unable to get off the bottom of the tank without swimming vigorously, and in extreme cases may be unable to keep themselves upright. It is important to note that in some species (notably hawkfishes and most blennies) the swimbladder is poorly developed or absent. Such fishes must swim energetically to hold position in the water. This is normal and not related to any problem.

External parasites

Very occasionally fishes will be affected by parasitic copepods or isopods, small crustaceans that attach to the skin and suck blood from the fish. These can be removed, as in the wild, by cleaner shrimps or fishes that perform the same function.

Gut parasites

Most wild-caught fishes probably harbor parasitic worms within their digestive systems. Usually these do not seem to cause problems, but in some species they appear to lead to a wasting syndrome, where the fish, despite apparently feeding well, becomes thinner and thinner until it dies. This phenomenon is commonly observed in *Valenciennea* gobies and in some wrasses. It may be that in the wild these species feed more or less continuously, obtaining enough

food to feed both themselves and their parasites, but in the aquarium this is not possible and the parasites get the available food at the expense of their hosts.

It is possible to use worming compounds designed for cats and dogs to treat fishes, but this requires some ingenuity in establishing the correct dose and persuading the fishes to take their medicine! It is far better simply to avoid buying affected fishes. When choosing fishes that are likely to be affected, it is best to observe them at the dealer's shop over a couple of weeks. If they stay looking sleek and plump, they are probably safe to buy, but if they visibly lose weight over this period, they are likely to waste away rapidly and should not be purchased.

Catching fishes in the reef aquarium

Although it is best (and usually essential) to treat diseased fishes in a separate hospital tank rather than in the reef aquarium, catching fishes to transfer them is often difficult. Most reef aquariums contain many rocks and invertebrates, which make wielding a net very difficult and provide fishes with plenty of hiding places. In some aquariums, fishes may become so tame that they will simply swim into a net (particularly if there is food on offer), but in most cases catching them is much trickier, perhaps involving the removal of most of the rocks and invertebrates from the tank.

Left: *This emaciated canary blenny* (Meiacanthus oulanensis) *may be suffering from gut parasites.*

CATCHING FISHES IN THE REEF AQUARIUM

Select a clear plastic bag (sized appropriately for the target fish) and a length of fishing line—nylon monofilament of at least 22 lb. (10 kg) breaking strain (for stiffness rather than strength) is best.

Thread the fishing line through a series of holes punched close to the open end of the bag, and then through a loop to form a drawstring.

Position the bag horizontally (with the open end to one side) on the base of the tank, weighted down with small pieces of rock or some sand to prevent it from floating away. The stiff fishing line holds the mouth of the bag open.

Place some food in the bag, and retire to a few feet away, holding on to the end of the fishing line. When the fish swims into the bag, pull sharply on the fishing line to close the mouth of the bag and catch the fish.

This method may take some patience: It might be a day or so before the target fish ventures into the bag—some species are more suspicious than others—but if the trap is left in place, and food placed into it regularly, even the most wary fishes will eventually be lured in.

Right: *Once trapped, fish can be transferred easily to a treatment tank, with minimum disruption to the display aquarium.*

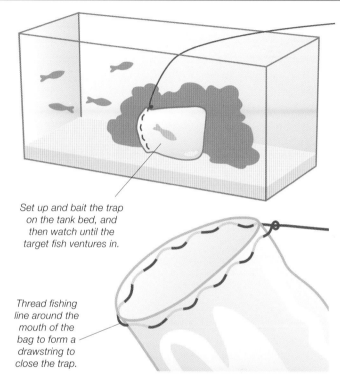

Set up and bait the trap on the tank bed, and then watch until the target fish ventures in.

Thread fishing line around the mouth of the bag to form a drawstring to close the trap.

The best method is to use a trap. Fish traps are commercially available, but you can make one quite simply following the instructions in the panel.

Disease prevention and quarantine

Rather than have to deal with disease problems in the display aquarium, it is far better to try to prevent them. Most diseases occur when fishes are stressed: This may be caused by problems with water quality, bullying by tankmates, and unsuitable environments, all of which are easily prevented. One classic cause of white spot outbreaks is sudden chilling, so ensuring temperature stability is a simple but highly effective way of minimizing disease outbreaks.

One particularly stressful time for fishes is the first few weeks in the aquarium. For wild-caught fishes, this period follows being captured and imported, then residing briefly in wholesalers' and dealers' tanks before being added to an aquarium that usually has established residents (that may initially resent the newcomer). For tank-bred fishes, the adjustment process is shorter and simpler, but the later stages are much the same.

Stress during this period can be reduced by quarantining new fishes. For this you will require a separate aquarium, but it need only be small and simple. A tank measuring 24 x 15 x 12 in. (60 x 38 x 30 cm) is adequate in most cases. Keep it running continuously—if necessary it can be used for treating sick fishes when not quarantining new ones. All that is needed is a simple aquarium with a heater-thermostat,

Above: Plastic pipe provides shelter in quarantine or treatment tanks, without interfering with any treatment.

Quarantine tank

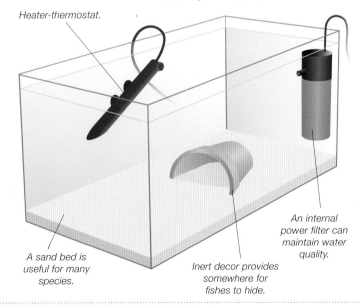

Heater-thermostat.

An internal power filter can maintain water quality.

A sand bed is useful for many species.

Inert decor provides somewhere for fishes to hide.

an internal power filter providing biological filtration (matured before the tank is used), a thin bed of sand, and some inert shelter (such as flowerpots or plastic pipe). New fishes can be placed in such a tank for a few weeks. If they are about to develop infections, they will usually do so in the quarantine tank, where the problem can be treated easily and there is no risk of infecting other fishes. Even if no problems occur, a few weeks in a quiet environment with no competition will allow new fishes to get over their journey from the reef to the aquarium before entering the hurly-burly of a display tank.

Below: A quarantine tank gives newly arrived fishes a chance to recover from their journey. Even so, once in the home aquarium they will need time to settle in.

Stocking levels

▶ The number of fishes an aquarium can accommodate is governed indirectly by the size of the tank. Ultimately, the capacity of an aquarium to support fishes and other animals is determined by two main factors, namely the availability of oxygen in the water, and the ability of the filtration system to process the waste products of the inhabitants, preventing them from building up to toxic levels. Although marine fishes need high levels of oxygen, in practice it is the latter factor that limits the stocking capacity of marine aquariums.

It is commonly recommended that reef aquariums should be stocked only very lightly with fishes, with fewer and/or smaller fishes than could be kept in a fish-only tank of the same size. This recommendation is primarily based on the fact that higher water quality is required by more invertebrates than is the case for most marine fishes. However, it makes rather outdated assumptions about the efficiency of biological filtration systems; it was probably correct in the days of undergravel filters and inefficient protein skimmers. In contrast, modern systems for running reef aquariums, based on live rock and powerful skimmers, can support quite a heavy fish load, and certainly no less than that of a fish-only system.

The fish-holding capacity of an aquarium is usually expressed in terms of the total length of fish (including tail fins, long noses, etc., as applicable) that can be kept in a certain volume of water. One good guideline is 2 in. (5 cm) fish length per 5 gal. (20 L) of tank

Above: Common clowns, shown here being added to an aquarium, are small enough to be kept in all but the tiniest tanks.

capacity. This generally works quite well, although it is better when considered in terms of smaller fishes than large ones. (Two 4-in. [10 cm] fishes generally add up to less weight of fish than one 8-in. [20 cm] specimen.) Nor does it apply to what might be termed "gross feeders"—predators such as eels or groupers, for example, that eat large meals and produce correspondingly large peaks of biological wastes.

It is a good idea to build up to this maximum stock level over a few months, perhaps leaving an interval of two weeks or thereabouts between successive additions of fishes. This allows the aquarium ecosystem (and not just the bacteria that process waste products) to adjust itself to the increase in biological load resulting from each new fish. Exceptions to this are when pairs, groups or shoals of fish need to be added; these should always be introduced to the aquarium together.

This 3-in. (8 cm) juvenile emperor angel looks small and easy to accommodate.

But as a 16-in (40 cm) adult it will need a very spacious aquarium. Always check how large fishes will grow before you buy them.

Fish size versus tank size

If an ultimate stocking level of 2 in. (5 cm) length of fish per 5 gal. (20 L) of tank capacity is taken to its logical extreme, it would suggest that, for example, a 50-gal. (200 L) tank could house a fish 20 in. (50 cm) long. As a typical 50-gal. (200 L) tank might be 48 in. (120 cm) long, 18 in. (45 cm) deep, and only 15 in. (38 cm) from front to back, this would be clearly absurd, as the 20-in. (50 cm) fish would not be able to turn around. For reasons of fish welfare (and, less importantly, the appearance of the tank; fishes that are too big for their aquarium look silly) it is obviously necessary to think not just in terms of the total stocking capacity, but also about the maximum size of fishes that a given tank can hold. This is not something that can be absolutely definitive, as different species vary greatly in their activity levels, but for "average" fishes it is possible to provide some guidelines that will ensure reasonable swimming space.

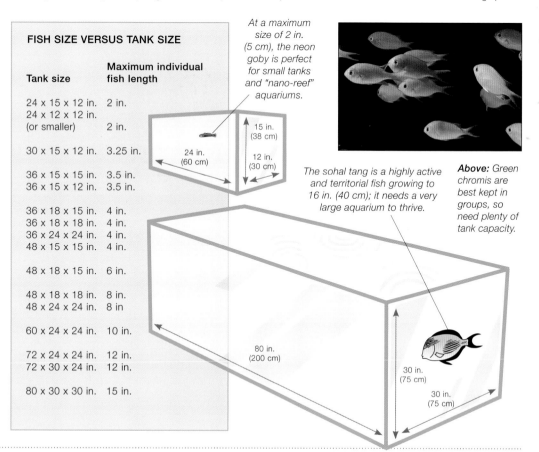

FISH SIZE VERSUS TANK SIZE

Tank size	Maximum individual fish length
24 x 15 x 12 in. 24 x 12 x 12 in. (or smaller)	2 in. 2 in.
30 x 15 x 12 in.	3.25 in.
36 x 15 x 15 in. 36 x 15 x 12 in.	3.5 in. 3.5 in.
36 x 18 x 15 in. 36 x 18 x 18 in. 36 x 24 x 24 in. 48 x 15 x 15 in.	4 in. 4 in. 4 in. 4 in.
48 x 18 x 15 in.	6 in.
48 x 18 x 18 in. 48 x 24 x 24 in.	8 in. 8 in
60 x 24 x 24 in.	10 in.
72 x 24 x 24 in. 72 x 30 x 24 in.	12 in. 12 in.
80 x 30 x 30 in.	15 in.

At a maximum size of 2 in. (5 cm), the neon goby is perfect for small tanks and "nano-reef" aquariums.

24 in. (60 cm)

15 in. (38 cm)

12 in. (30 cm)

The sohal tang is a highly active and territorial fish growing to 16 in. (40 cm); it needs a very large aquarium to thrive.

80 in. (200 cm)

30 in. (75 cm)

30 in. (75 cm)

Above: Green chromis are best kept in groups, so need plenty of tank capacity.

How fishes can be useful

▶ Many fishes are not just decorative inhabitants of the reef aquarium but are actually useful, helping the aquarium to run successfully. These fishes fit into two categories: algae grazers and predators of pests.

Algae grazers
Reef tanks can be easily overwhelmed by nuisance algae. Invertebrates can be used to graze algae, but herbivorous fishes are generally more effective, keeping the aquarium looking good and making it a better environment for corals.

Tangs are probably the most important algae grazers in the aquarium. Different tang species eat different types of algae, and eat it in different ways. *Zebrasoma* tangs feed primarily on filamentous

algae (although they will eat many other types), using clipper-like mouthparts to snip off fronds—a method of feeding also used by many *Acanthurus* species. *Ctenochaetus* tangs, in contrast, scrape films of microalgae from hard surfaces, using the comblike teeth that line their large lips.

Tangs make great reef aquarium fishes, but do have some limitations. They are generally large (the smallest species can grow to around 6 in. [15 cm]) and so need spacious tanks, and some can be very territorial. As a family, they also tend to be quite prone to white spot *(Cryptocaryon)* infections.

Below: Using their comblike teeth, Ctenochaetus *species, such as this kole tang, graze algal films and detritus from rocks and sand.*

Rabbitfishes are close relatives of the tangs, and like them are voracious algae grazers. Like the tangs, they tend to be large, the smaller species reaching 6 in. (20 cm), and most growing to around 16 in. (40 cm). Rabbitfishes are not as safe with all sessile invertebrates as tangs. Unlike tangs, they are typically very disease resistant, but have the disadvantage of having venomous spines.

Blennies are often useful grazers for smaller aquariums, as many of the herbivorous members of this family are much smaller than tangs, ranging from 2 to 6 in. (5 to 15 cm). Examples include the bicolor blenny *(Ecsenius bicolor)* and most other *Ecsenius* species, the algae blenny *(Salarias fasciatus)* and the "flymo" blennies *(Blenniella* species). Unfortunately, some blennies are more likely to bother invertebrates, and less willing to eat prepared foods than tangs are.

Angelfishes often eat algae but, with a few exceptions, are generally a risky prospect in the reef aquarium. Some of the *Centropyge* species can be safe, useful grazers, but even within a species individuals seem to vary greatly in their willingness to eat different types of algae.

Gobies are not generally thought of as grazers, but there are a few herbivorous species. The best known are *Amblygobius* species, including the court jester *(Amblygobius rainfordi)* and the yellow-stripe, or Hector's, goby

(Amblygobius hectori). These are small (2–2.5 in [5–6 cm]), quite shy fishes that need peaceful companions and live rock and sand beds to provide algae to graze.

Pest predators—flatworms
Almost all reef aquariums are home to flatworms, which are usually unobtrusive and harmless. However, some species can cause problems. The red flatworm (Convolutriloba retrogemma) is one example. This species can proliferate in well-lit, well-fed aquariums and often congregates on top of corals, irritating them, shading their tissues, and possibly feeding on them. There are also some species that are definitely parasites or predators of corals, and these too can proliferate in the aquarium.

Several species of wrasses eat flatworms. These include Halichoeres species, such as the banana wrasse (H. chrysus), the silver-belly wrasse (H.

Above: The copperband butterfly eats Aiptasia anemones, which can be a nuisance in the reef aquarium.

leucoxanthus), the radiant wrasse (H. iridis), and the pinstripe wrasse (H. melanurus). Pseudocheilinus species, such as the pajama wrasse (P. hexataenia), and some fairy wrasses (Cirrhilabrus species) will also eat at least some types of flatworms.

Aiptasia anemones can be a real pest in the reef aquarium, proliferating rapidly and damaging neighboring invertebrates. Fortunately there is a fish that is generally safe in the reef aquarium and that will usually eat Aiptasia. This is the copperband butterfly (Chelmon rostratus). It is not an easy species to keep, and grows quite large, so is not suitable for all aquariums.

Parasitic snails Tridacna species clams are parasitized by a range

THE IMPORTANCE OF GRAZERS

Some years ago, marine biologists tried an interesting experiment on a coral reef. They put cages over some small areas of reef, the idea being to prevent predators such as butterflyfishes from gaining access to corals. One of their key interests was in the growth rate of the corals—would they grow faster without predation? The results surprised them. Rather than corals growing faster inside the cages, the corals were killed, overgrown by algae. The cages had not just excluded coral predators—more important, they had also excluded algae-grazing fishes.

This shows the huge importance of algae-grazing fishes to the reef environment, and the reef aquarium is no different—without grazing, reef tanks can easily be overwhelmed by algae.

of small snails that suck their body fluids. These include pyramidellid snails, such as Turbonilla and Tathrella species, among others. Some are very small and difficult to remove by hand, and many of them can multiply rapidly, endangering the lives of their hosts. A number of wrasses, however, will eat these snails, including some of the species that also eat flatworms. These include the pajama wrasse (Pseudocheilinus hexataenia) and various Halichoeres species.

Part Two

Fish Profiles

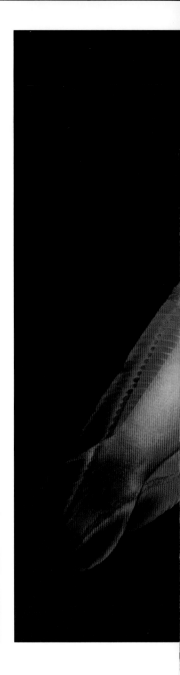

▶ With their beautiful forms and colors, and their fascinating behavior, fishes add the finishing touch to any reef aquarium, and can have a huge impact on the interest of the tank. They can really bring the aquarium to life, but they do need to be chosen with care. We hope this section will provide the information necessary for any enthusiast to find the very best fishes for their reef aquarium.

This part of the book is a guide to choosing fishes for the reef aquarium. The 180 fishes described are far from constituting an exhaustive list, but the selected species are known to make reliable inhabitants for the reef aquarium. In most cases, these species satisfy the most stringent definitions of being "reef aquarium safe." Where this is not the case, and an aquarium that is more specialized than a generalized reef tank (perhaps including a more restricted selection of invertebrates) is required, this is noted.

▶ *A pair of firefishes hover in midwater.*

Damselfishes and clownfishes

The damselfishes are famed among fishkeepers for two things: their hardiness and their aggression. This stereotype holds true for some species, but it is far from being universally correct. While many damselfishes are very aggressive—to the point where in the wild they will attack divers who get too close to their territories—there are also more peaceful species. Also, not all damsels are quite as hardy as is commonly supposed. However, many of them are very colorful, and one specialized group, the clownfishes, are very important as aquarium fishes. Here we look at a selection of clownfishes before considering some other good damselfishes for the aquarium.

PROFILE

Clownfishes are among the most popular of all marine aquarium fishes, although two species—the common clown *Amphiprion ocellaris* and the percula clown *A. percula*—account for the vast majority of those kept. They are real icons of the coral reef, particularly since the animated film *Finding Nemo* was produced. They were, however, famous before the film came along, primarily for their relationships with large sea anemones. Clownfishes live in pairs or small groups among the tentacles of the anemones, immune to the stings that would kill most other small fishes. In return for the protection of the anemone's stinging tentacles, clownfishes guard their anemones from predators such as butterflyfishes, and the waste products of the clownfishes may provide food for their hosts.

Clownfishes are notable in the marine aquarium world because, as a family, they are relatively easy to breed in captivity—although raising the young is a tricky process requiring considerable dedication from those hobby fishkeepers who attempt it. As a result of commercial breeding operations most clownfishes in the aquarium trade are tank-bred. As tank-bred clownfishes are, in most

Price guide

★	Up to $16
★★	$16–32
★★★	$32–48
★★★★	$48–80
★★★★★	$80–120

Amphiprion species

Clownfishes

species, much hardier than wild-caught fishes (a difference that is particularly extreme in the case of the most common species, *A. ocellaris* and *A. percula*), this makes clownfishes much easier to keep than they would otherwise be.

Clownfishes should ideally be kept in pairs in the aquarium. Clownfishes begin life as "males" (although they are not reproductively active at this stage). In the wild, they tend to live in groups in sea anemones, with one larger breeding pair and several smaller individuals. The dominant fish in the group becomes the female, and the next in the hierarchy the reproductive male. In the aquarium, groups of clownfishes do not work so well: The dominant pair tend to bully the other members of the group. Pairs are therefore a better bet; in most cases, pairs can be formed by simply adding

▲ *Clownfishes frolick among the tentacles of a sea anemone—a very appealing sight but hard to reproduce in the aquarium.*

two small juvenile fishes to the aquarium. These are usually quick to establish which is the dominant individual, and this becomes a female, the other becoming a male. The exception to this is the maroon clown, *Premnas biaculeatus*, where pair formation is much more difficult.

Amphiprion species

Small clownfishes

The smaller *Amphiprion* species make perfect fishes for reef aquariums—provided that they are tank-bred individuals. Such fishes are ideal for beginners to marine fishkeeping, but are also very popular with more experienced enthusiasts thanks to their beauty, their appealing personalities, and their great hardiness. A number of different color morphs of common and percula clowns are available. Although suitable for small tanks, they are usually extroverted enough not to get lost from view in large systems. Aquarium spawnings of common and percula clowns are frequent, especially in larger tanks.

WHERE do they live in the wild?
In sheltered lagoons or on reefs, from shallow water to depths of 100 ft. (30 m), depending on species. Associate with a range of large sea anemones, the range of anemone species depending on the clownfish species. Seldom seen far from host anemones.

WHAT aquarium environment?
No special requirements beyond a specific place that can be adopted as a home. Do not require anemones in the aquarium. No particular requirements with respect to lighting.

WHAT do they eat?
Feed readily on almost all aquarium foods. Should be fed at least twice daily.

HOW hardy?
Captive-bred specimens are extremely hardy and seldom have disease problems.

HOW compatible with other fishes?
Generally peaceful toward unrelated species, except when defending clutches of eggs. Will fight with other clownfishes. Common and percula clowns are robust characters that will live happily with larger, more boisterous fishes (with the obvious exception of species that will eat them) whereas skunk clowns prefer quieter companions.

HOW compatible with invertebrates?
Harmless to all invertebrates, with the exception that they may use some corals as substitute sea anemones: In most cases this is tolerated by the coral, but if not, the coral (or the clownfish) should be removed.

WHAT do they cost?
★☆☆☆☆   ★★★☆☆
Prices are for captive-bred fish, except *A. akallopisos,* which is the most expensive (★★★).

Percula clown
Amphiprion percula

Very similar to the common clown, the percula clown in its typical "wild-type" form tends to have heavier black markings around its white stripes. This difference is not so clear in the various tank-bred color morphs. Black and white percula clowns are occasionally found in the wild. In the aquarium, this species usually prefers to live close to the surface (even when not about to be fed), whereas common clowns tend to reside deeper in the water. Percula clowns also tend to be more aggressive than common clowns.

WHAT size? 2.5 in (6.5 cm)
WHAT min size tank? 16 x 12 x 12 in. (40 x 30 x 30 cm)
WHERE is it from? Western Pacific Ocean from northern Great Barrier Reef to Solomon Islands and Vanuatu. Associated with the anemones Heteractis magnifica, Heteractis crispa, and Stichodactyla gigantea.

Common clown
Amphiprion ocellaris

This species is widely available in tank-bred form, in a number of different color morphs, including black and white; orange, black, and white; and various shades of orange ranging from almost yellow to nearly red. It should be noted, however, that the color can change with age. Tank-bred common clowns seldom achieve the full size of their wild counterparts.

WHAT size? 3 in. (8 cm)
WHAT min size tank? 16 x 12 x 12 in. (40 x 30 x 30 cm)
WHERE is it from? Indo-West Pacific – eastern Indian Ocean to Taiwan; typically associated with the anemones Heteractis magnifica, Stichodactyla gigantea, and Stichodactyla mertensii.

Amphiprion species
Small clownfishes

Pink skunk clown
Amphiprion perideraion

The most commonly available of the skunk clowns — in both wild and tank-bred forms — this is a very peaceful species. Aquarium spawnings are rare, and tend to occur only in larger tanks, or when the pair of clowns are kept on their own. Tank-bred individuals tend to be smaller than wild ones.

WHAT size? *4 in. (10 cm)*
WHAT min size tank? *30 x 15 x 12 in. (75 x 38 x 30 cm)*
WHERE is it from? *Western Pacific Ocean over a wide range from Thailand to Samoa and Tonga, from the Ryukyu Islands to the Great Barrier Reef; most commonly associated with the anemone* Heteractis magnifica, *but also found with* Heteractis crispa, Macrodactyla doreensis, *and* Stichodactyla gigantea.

Skunk clown
Amphiprion akallopisos

The skunk clown is not a common sight in aquarium shops and can be difficult to find in tank-bred form. It is a very attractive species, and worth seeking out for those interested in keeping an unusual clownfish species. It is quite shy and seldom spawns in the aquarium.

WHAT size? *4 in. (10 cm)*
WHAT min size tank? *36 x 18 x 15 in. (90 x 45 x 38 cm)*
WHERE is it from? *Indian Ocean (East Africa, Madagascar, Comoro Islands, and Seychelles) to Indonesia. Associated with the anemones* Heteractis magnifica *and* Stichodactyla mertensii.

Yellow skunk clown
Amphiprion sandaracinos

With its single, broad, white stripe along the back, among the skunk clowns this species best earns its common name. This species is an infrequent import, and is also hard to find in tank-bred form. Like other skunk clowns it is quite shy and should not be kept with boisterous species.

WHAT size? *4 in. (10 cm)*
WHAT min size tank? *36 x 18 x 15 in. (90 x 45 x 38 cm)*

WHERE is it from? *Western Pacific Ocean from Christmas Island and Western Australia to the Ryukyu Islands, Taiwan, the Philippines, New Guinea, and the Solomon Islands. Associated with the anemones* Heteractis crispa *and* Stichodactyla mertensii.

Amphiprion species

Fire and tomato clowns

PROFILE

Large, beautiful, and active, this group of clowns is sometimes referred to as the "tomato complex" because of the close relationship of the other species to *Amphiprion frenatus* and includes two species very rare in the aquarium trade, the Australian clown (*A. rubrocinctus*) and McCulloch's clown (*A. mccullochi*). With the exception of these latter two species, about which little is known, these clowns are hardy (reasonably so even in wild form), easy to keep and to breed—but can be very territorial.

WHERE do they live in the wild?

Found in lagoons, shallow bays, and on reefs, ranging down to around 60 ft. (18 m) depth. Found in pairs or groups associated with a range of large sea anemones. Venture farther away from their hosts than smaller clowns.

WHAT aquarium environment?

Not fussy with respect to aquarium layout, but prefer a shell or other object to use as a home and, potentially, a spawning site. Anemones are not required in the aquarium.

WHAT do they eat?

Will eat all aquarium foods. Should be fed at least twice daily.

HOW hardy?

Even wild-caught individuals are usually relatively hardy, and tank-bred fishes are virtually bomb-proof. It should be noted that if the saddleback clown (*Amphiprion ephippium*) does get a parasitic infection, it cannot be treated with copper medications, which are highly toxic to this species.

HOW compatible with other fishes?

Highly territorial, particularly toward other clownfishes, and will even attack fishkeepers' hands. Should be kept in pairs—either bought as such or as two small juveniles added to the aquarium together. Best kept with other large, boisterous species.

HOW compatible with invertebrates?

May adopt corals as a home, and (because of their large size) may sometimes inadvertently damage them. Very large individuals may eat small shrimps.

WHAT do they cost?

★★☆☆☆   ★★★★☆

◁ **Saddleback clown**
Amphiprion ephippium

This is the only clownfish species that always lacks white stripes as an adult, although a band is present on the head of juveniles. The dark mark on the flanks that gives this species its common name appears as a dot in juveniles and gradually expands as the fish grows; in a mature adult it may extend into the tail and the rear of the dorsal fin.

WHAT size? *5.5 in (14 cm)*
WHAT min size tank? *48 x 18 x 18 in. (120 x 45 x 45 cm)*
WHERE is it from? *Eastern Indian Ocean: Andaman and Nicobar Islands, Thailand, Malaysia, Java, and Sumatra. Associates with the anemones Entacmaea quadricolor and Heteractis crispa.*

Tomato clown
Amphiprion frenatus

Big and bold, tomato clowns are among the hardiest of clownfish but are also highly territorial. Juveniles have three white stripes, but only the one on the head persists into adulthood. Females develop black flanks with age, but their head, fins, and tail remain their base color, which ranges from burnt orange to bright red; males lack the black on the flanks. This is one of the easiest clowns to breed in captivity.

WHAT size? 5.5 in. (14 cm)
WHAT min size tank? 48 x 18 x 18 in. (120 x 45 x 45 cm)
WHERE is it from? Western Pacific Ocean: Gulf of Thailand to Palau, north to southern Japan, south to Java. Associates with the anemone Entacmaea quadricolor.

Fire clown
Amphiprion melanopus

Dazzling bright orange with velvety black flanks and a vivid white or bluish stripe behind the head, this is a beautiful but highly territorial species—and when pairs are preparing to spawn, the fishkeeper can be the target of their aggression. There is considerable geographic color variation in this species: Fire clowns from Fiji and Tonga lack the black on the flanks; those from the Coral Sea lack white bands.

WHAT size? 5 in. (12 cm)
WHAT min size tank? 48 x 18 x 18 in. (120 x 45 x 45 cm)
WHERE is it from? Pacific Ocean, from Bali in Indonesia to the Philippines, New Guinea, Queensland, Solomon Islands, Vanuatu, Fiji, Tonga, Samoa, to Marshall Islands. Usually associated with the anemone Entacmaea quadricolor, less commonly with Heteractis crispa or Heteractis magnifica.

▼ A young tomato clown nestles among the tentacles of an anemone.

Sebae and polymnus clowns

PROFILE

The sebae and polymnus clowns are beautiful fishes but are among the most difficult clownfishes to keep in the aquarium. Seldom available in tank-bred form, they are delicate fishes, very susceptible to parasitic infections and—unusually for clowns—very nervous and jittery. As such, they are fishes only for those who are prepared to provide the special care they require. They seldom spawn in the aquarium. Their second white band, across the middle of the body, is saddle-shaped in *Amphiprion polymnus* and a sweeping S-shape in *A. sebae*.

WHERE do they live in the wild?

In shallow lagoons, silty bays, and harbors, in pairs or groups associated with large sea anemones.

WHAT aquarium environment?

No special requirements in the aquarium, other than a coral, large empty shell, or similar that they can adopt as a home. Because of their nervous nature, the tank should be situated in a quiet spot.

WHAT do they eat?

Will eat all aquarium foods. Should be fed at least twice daily.

HOW hardy?

Very delicate, particularly in wild-caught form. Susceptible to parasitic infections and need expert care. Benefit from extended quarantine before being introduced to a display aquarium.

HOW compatible with other fishes?

Require quiet companions, as they tend to be very nervous.

HOW compatible with invertebrates?

Usually safe with all invertebrates; may occasionally adopt corals as homes and may very rarely damage them.

WHAT do they cost?

★★★★☆ ★★★★★

▼ *The orange form of* Amphiprion polymnus *shares a large carpet anemone with domino damsels,* Dascyllus trimaculatus.

Sebae clown
Amphiprion sebae

This is a very beautiful fish, but difficult to keep. In most areas it is only rarely available in tank-bred form. Juveniles are yellow but usually develop brown markings as they age, although in some areas adults remain all-yellow, and in other areas they are almost completely black. The tail fin is yellow, unlike in A. polymnus, which is otherwise very similar.

WHAT size? *6.5 in. (16 cm)*
WHAT min size tank? *48 x 24 x 24 in. (120 x 60 x 60 cm)*
WHERE is it from? *Indian Ocean: from the Arabian peninsula, the coasts of India and Sri Lanka, the Maldives, Andaman Islands, Java and Sumatra. Associates with the anemone* Stichodactyla haddoni.

▲ Amphiprion polymnus *is an unusual but very delicate clownfish.*

Polymnus clown
Amphiprion polymnus

This species is very beautiful, with its combination of velvety black, bright white, and vivid yellow, but it is difficult to find in tank-bred form. Two forms occur, the usual one with a yellow face and belly, and a black-and-white form. The tail in this species is dark, often with a white edge, not yellow as in the sebae clown.

WHAT size? *5 in. (13 cm)*
WHAT min size tank? *48 x 18 x 18 in. (120 x 45 x 45 cm)*
WHERE is it from? *Western Pacific Ocean: from southern Japan, China, Taiwan, the Philippines, Vietnam, and Thailand to New Guinea, the Northern Territories in Australia, Indonesia and the Solomon Islands. Associates with the anemones* Stichodactyla haddoni *and* Heteractis crispa.

Amphiprion clarkii

Clark's clown

PROFILE

Clark's clowns are among the easiest of the large clowns to find in tank-bred form, and are typically very easy to keep—and to breed in the aquarium. Adult *Amphiprion clarkii* are highly variable in color, ranging from almost completely yellow through various shades of brown to almost black. Although they typically have three white bands, the one closest to the tail is sometimes missing. These clowns are part of a "species complex" that includes seven similar species, many of which are not easy to distinguish from *A. clarkii*—although most of the other species in the complex are far less common in the aquarium trade, being only rarely imported as wild fishes and hardly ever available in tank-bred form. There are exceptions, such as the Red Sea clown *A. bicinctus*, although this is a more distinctive species.

WHAT size?
6 in. (15 cm)

WHERE is it from?
Indian Ocean and western Pacific Ocean: from Persian Gulf to Western Australia, to Taiwan, southern Japan, and Melanesia and Micronesia.

WHERE does it live in the wild?
In lagoons and on outer reef slopes, in pairs or in small groups, associated with a wide range of large sea anemones: *Cryptodendrum adhaesivum; Entacmaea quadricolor; Heteractis malu; Heteractis aurora; Heteractis magnifica; Heteractis crispa; Macrodactyla doreensis; Stichodactyla haddoni; Stichodactyla gigantea;* and *Stichodactyla mertensii.*

WHAT aquarium environment?
No particular requirements other than a place (a coral, old clam shell, or similar) that it can adopt as a home.

WHAT minimum size tank?
48 x 18 x 18 in. (120 x 45 x 45 cm)

WHAT does it eat?
Will eat all aquarium foods: Feed at least twice a day.

HOW hardy?
Tank-bred individuals are very hardy; wild-caught fishes are delicate and very prone to parasitic infections.

HOW compatible with other fishes?
These are very bold fishes and can be kept with large or boisterous tankmates: Small or shy species may be intimidated by them.

HOW compatible with invertebrates?
Usually completely safe with all invertebrates, although large individuals may eat small shrimps. If they adopt a coral as a home (which they sometimes do), it could be damaged, but this is rare.

WHAT does it cost?
★★★☆☆

OTHER LARGE CLOWNS

There are many other species of large clownfishes, but most are rarely seen in the aquarium trade and even more rarely in tank-bred form—in some cases this is because they live outside the usual areas in which aquarium fish are collected, but even when the species are available, given the usually delicate nature of wild-caught clowns, getting breeding programs established requires considerable dedication. The species described here are available at least intermittently, or in the case of Clark's clownfish, fairly frequently.

Amphiprion bicinctus

Red Sea clown

PROFILE

This is a beautiful species, often with much more yellow on the body than other clowns—some individuals are completely yellow apart from the two white bands. The fins are often larger than those in other clowns, too. This is a relatively uncommon species in both wild and tank-bred form, but the latter in particular are worth seeking out, as Red Sea clowns are such attractive fishes. They are more difficult to breed in the aquarium than many other clowns.

WHAT size?
5.5 in. (14 cm)

WHERE is it from?
Red Sea and the Chagos Archipelago in the western Indian Ocean.

WHERE does it live in the wild?
In lagoons and on seaward reefs, in pairs or small groups, in association with the sea anemones *Entacmaea quadricolor; Heteractis aurora; Heteractis magnifica; Heteractis crispa;* and *Stichodactyla gigantea.*

WHAT aquarium environment?
No specific requirements other than a place to use as a home.

WHAT minimum size tank?
48 x 18 x 18 in. (120 x 45 x 45 cm)

WHAT does it eat?
Will eat any frozen or dry foods. Feed at least twice daily.

HOW hardy?
Tank-bred fishes are very hardy; wild-caught individuals are delicate and need careful quarantine. Do not tolerate copper treatment of parasitic infections (to which wild fishes are very susceptible).

HOW compatible with other fishes?
Not usually aggressive toward unrelated species, but territorial; will defend their home area in the tank.

HOW compatible with invertebrates?
Usually safe with all invertebrates; sometimes adopts corals as a home and, rarely, may inadvertently damage them. May eat vary small shrimps.

WHAT does it cost?
★★★★★

◀ *Rarely seen for sale, and not easy to keep, the Red Sea clown is a beautiful fish for those who can provide the care it needs.*

Premnas biaculeatus

Maroon clown

PROFILE

The only non-*Amphiprion* clownfish, this species is easily distinguished from all other clowns by the spines on its gill covers. Males are usually much smaller than females (which are the largest of all clowns). Getting pairs to form in this species is more difficult than for other clownfishes: Maroon clowns are highly aggressive toward their own species and the struggle for dominance tends to overwhelm the instinct to form pairs; in most cases this species is best kept as a single specimen, but to form pairs there should be a large size difference between the potential partners so that the smaller fish will capitulate quickly and become (or remain) the male. Two forms of maroon clowns are found, one with white stripes, the other with yellow stripes.

▶ *The yellow-striped form of the maroon clown is less often seen than the white-striped form, and is highly prized.*

WHAT size?
7 in. (17 cm)

WHERE is it from?
Indian Ocean and western Pacific Ocean: India, Burma, Thailand, Malaysia, Indonesia, the Philippines, Solomon Islands, Vanuatu, and northern Queensland in Australia.

WHERE does it live in the wild?
Mainly found in lagoons and sheltered coastal waters, occasionally on seaward reefs, usually in pairs, associated with the anemone *Entacmaea quadricolor*.

WHAT aquarium environment?
No specific needs in the aquarium, other than a place to use as a home.

WHAT minimum size tank?
48 x 24 x 24 in. (120 x 60 x 60 cm)

WHAT does it eat?
Will usually eat all frozen and dry foods. Feed at least twice a day.

HOW hardy?
Tank-bred individuals are hardy, but wild fishes are much more delicate.

HOW compatible with other fishes?
More territorial than most clowns, but not usually highly aggressive toward unrelated species provided they do not get too close to the clowns' home.

HOW compatible with invertebrates?
Usually safe with all invertebrates, although large individuals may eat very small shrimps. Sometimes chooses a coral as a home, and may inadvertently damage it.

WHAT does it cost?
★★★★☆ ★★★★★

◀ *The more common white-striped form of the maroon clown.*

Pomacentrus alleni

Allen's damsel

PROFILE

Pomacentrus damsels can be divided into two categories: omnivores, which graze algae and hunt small invertebrates on hard substrates, and planktivores that capture their food in the water column. The former are highly territorial, which makes sense given that they need to defend the area in which they feed, to the point where it can be difficult to keep them in the aquarium because they will attack almost any fish housed with them. Planktivorous species, such as the very attractive, shimmering blue Allen's damsel, are much more peaceable and a better bet for the aquarium.

WHAT size?
2.5 in. (6 cm)

WHERE is it from?
Eastern Indian Ocean: Thailand and Indonesia.

WHERE does it live in the wild?
Mainly found in areas of rubble and dead coral, often in small groups.

WHAT aquarium environment?
Some rocks and invertebrates to provide cover, plus plenty of open water.

WHAT minimum size tank?
24 x 15 x 12 in. (60 x 38 x 30 cm)

▼ *Allen's damsel is one of the more peaceful of this family.*

WHAT does it eat?
Will usually eat all small frozen and dry foods. Should be fed at least three times a day.

HOW hardy?
Very hardy.

HOW compatible with other fishes?
Reasonably peaceful, and can be kept with other peaceful fishes. Should not be kept with very aggressive tankmates. Can be kept in groups in larger aquariums.

HOW compatible with invertebrates?
Usually safe with all invertebrates.

WHAT does it cost?
★☆☆☆☆ ★★☆☆☆

Chromis viridis

Green chromis

Many of the 95 known *Chromis* species are unusual among the damselfishes in that they form large shoals that hover above the reef catching zooplankton. They can be kept in groups in the aquarium, and generally do best when kept in this way. The green chromis is typical of many of the *Chromis* species, although few are frequent imports—the very similar blackaxil chromis *(C. atripectoralis)* and the blue chromis *(C. cyanea)* are the most common. These fishes provide a wonderful display when kept in a large group in the reef aquarium. *Chromis* will sometimes spawn in the aquarium.

WHAT size?
3 in. (8 cm)

WHERE is it from?
Widely distributed from Red Sea, across Indian Ocean and Pacific Ocean to the Line Islands, Marquesas and Tuamato, north to Ryukyu Islands and south to New Caledonia.

WHERE does it live in the wild?
Mainly found over sheltered reef flats and lagoons, hovering in large shoals above *Acropora* branching stony corals.

▲ *The green chromis is a lively, pretty shoaling species, ideal for medium to large reef aquariums.*

WHAT aquarium environment?
No specific needs in the aquarium, but a reef aquarium with branching stony corals and strong water currents mimics their natural environment well.

WHAT minimum size tank?
36 x 18 x 18 in. (90 x 45 x 45 cm)

WHAT does it eat?
Will usually eat all small frozen and dry foods. Needs a vitamin-rich, varied diet in order to maintain its color. Should be fed at least three times a day.

HOW hardy?
Less hardy than many other damselfishes, but still generally a robust species, especially if not stressed by being kept with aggressive tankmates.

HOW compatible with other fishes?
Not a threat to other species, and may be intimidated by large or boisterous fishes. Can be kept in groups; these have dominance hierarchies and in small groups the weakest individuals will be bullied, so it is best to keep groups of at least seven fishes so that the aggression in the group can be dispersed among a larger number of fishes. Add all members of the group to the aquarium at the same time.

HOW compatible with invertebrates?
Usually safe with all invertebrates, although has been observed to bite tentacles off mushroom anemones, without doing permanent damage.

WHAT does it cost?
★☆☆☆☆ ★★☆☆☆

Chrysiptera species

Chrysiptera damsels

PROFILE

The *Chrysiptera* damsels are among the most beautiful of their family and some of the most suitable for the reef aquarium. With some exceptions they are not generally among the most aggressive damsels (although they are assertive and can usually hold their own with most tankmates).

WHERE do they live in the wild?

Many species are found in lagoons and over sheltered inshore reefs, typically in coral-rich areas. Some species range into deeper water, to depths of 66–100 ft. (20–30 m).

WHAT aquarium environment?

Prefer plenty of rocks and invertebrates; well suited to reef tanks with many caves and crevices.

WHAT do they eat?

Will eat all aquarium foods. Should be fed at least twice daily.

HOW hardy?

Very hardy.

HOW compatible with other fishes?

Species vary; most are reasonably peaceful and some can be kept in groups in larger tanks, but there are more aggressive species.

HOW compatible with invertebrates?

Usually harmless to all invertebrates.

WHAT do they cost?

★★☆☆☆   ★★★☆☆

Yellowtail blue damsel
Chrysiptera parasema

An old favorite marine aquarium fish, hardy and beautiful. By the standards of damselfishes, it is not particularly territorial and should not be kept with highly aggressive tankmates. It can be kept in pairs or small groups in medium-sized tanks, and will often spawn in the aquarium.

WHAT size? 3 in. (7 cm)
WHAT min size tank? 24 x 15 x 12 in. (60 x 38 x 30 cm)
WHERE is it from? Western Pacific Ocean: Solomon Islands, northern Papua New Guinea, the Philippines, Ryukyu Islands.

▽

▲ *The yellowtail blue damsel is one of the best* Chrysiptera *species for the aquarium.*

Fiji damsel
Chrysiptera taupou

One of the more aggressive Chrysiptera damsels, this species is best kept with larger, robust tankmates. It is a very attractive species and is common in the aquarium trade. It is best not kept with others of its own species, except in mated pairs.

WHAT size? 3 in. (8 cm)
WHAT min size tank? 30 x 15 x 12 in. (75 x 38 x 30 cm)
WHERE is it from? Western Pacific Ocean: Coral Sea (including Great Barrier Reef) to Samoa.

Starck's damsel
Chrysiptera starcki

This distinctively colored species is collected in deeper water than most other species and prefers tanks that do not have highly intense lighting. It is a moderately aggressive fish that should not be kept with shy or very small tankmates.

WHAT size? 3 in. (7 cm)
WHAT min size tank? 24 x 15 x 12 in. (60 x 38 x 30 cm)
WHERE is it from? Western Pacific Ocean: Ryukyu Islands to Taiwan and Queensland to New Caledonia.

▽

Anthias, basses, grammas, forktails & dottybacks

▶ The diverse fishes featured in this section include some stunningly beautiful species that are ideal for the reef aquarium. They range from very hardy, easy-to-keep species such as the *Pseudochromis* dottybacks to the challenging *Pseudanthias* species; from the tiny forktails (*Assessor* species) to hefty *Serranus* basses; and from the peaceful grammas to the diminutive but highly aggressive *Pictichromis* species. These fishes are all safe to keep with all sessile invertebrates such as corals, anemones, and clams, but some pose a threat to shrimps, particularly small ones.

Price guide

★	$16–24
★★	$24–32
★★★	$32–48
★★★★	$48–64
★★★★★	$64–96

PROFILE

Anthias, or wreckfishes, are a very prominent feature of coral reefs in the Indian and Pacific Oceans, as they hover above the reef in often huge shoals, feeding on plankton. They are very beautiful but rather challenging as aquarium fishes. There are a number of factors that make them tricky to keep. First is their requirement for frequent feeding. In the wild, they feed in a "little and often" pattern, catching whatever the currents bring them. This is common among fishes that eat plankton, but in anthias it seems to be a stricter requirement than in other planktivores—the usual once or twice daily feeding routine in the home aquarium does not suit them. This may be why anthias often look much better in public aquariums and in aquarium dealers' shops, where they can be given the frequent small feeds they need, than in home aquariums. Having a refugium in the aquarium system, to provide a constant trickle of small live foods, can be very useful when keeping these species.

The second main challenge with anthias is their social structure. The large shoals seen in the wild are made up of smaller groups of fishes, each consisting of a male and several females. Males are often larger than females and have different coloration. Anthias appear to begin life as females, and within a group of females the dominant fish will become male. This creates a competitive situation within groups of females. Males are even more aggressive toward each other, as they compete to spawn with the females. This means that in the aquarium, it is best to keep either single individuals or groups of eight or more, and with only a single male among them. The ideal situation is probably one male and eight or more females. Some anthias are also aggressive toward other planktivorous fishes.

Although some anthias are highly aggressive, others are very shy, particularly when first introduced to the aquarium. If these latter species are kept with boisterous tankmates, they may refuse to come out from cover even to feed, which, given their requirement for frequent meals, can rapidly prove fatal.

Anthias are also quite demanding in terms of their aquarium environment; in the wild they swim over the reef in strong currents and clear, well-oxygenated water, and these

Below: Anthias form large shoals, made up of smaller groups of several females and a single male, hovering over coral reefs.

Anthias species

conditions should be provided in their tank. Some species come from quite deep water, and these require relatively subdued lighting.

In summary, anthias are fishes best left to experienced fishkeepers. The many different species vary widely in their ease or otherwise of husbandry; however tempting dazzling anthias are in an aquarium dealer's tanks, it is essential to do some background research on the particular species on offer before committing to a purchase. Those species described here are among the more straightforward to keep.

WHERE do they live in the wild?

Typically found swimming in open water over coral or rocky reefs, or around drop-offs and reef edges, typically in strong currents, feeding on zooplankton. Different species may be found at depths ranging from 6.5 to 330 ft. (2–100 m). Found in shoals of varying size, depending on species; sometimes mixed shoals are found. Some species are found around caves and overhangs.

WHAT aquarium environment?

Large expanses of open water, but some rocks or invertebrates to provide shelter. Some species require more caves and overhangs. Provide strong currents, high

oxygen levels, and high-quality, nutrient-poor water. Deep-water species require relatively low light levels. Very active, so need larger tanks than their size would suggest.

WHAT do they eat?

Frozen crustaceans (brineshrimp, mysis, krill, and copepods) should form the mainstay of the diet, supplemented with frozen fish and lobster roe, and live brineshrimp. Occasionally learn to accept dry foods. Need frequent feeds, at least four or five small meals per day.

HOW hardy?

Species vary, but many are quite delicate. Species featured here are reasonably hardy provided their specific needs (particularly frequent feeds) are met.

HOW compatible with other fishes?

Species vary, but many are aggressive toward other

planktivorous fishes. Other fish that are not perceived as competitors are usually left alone. Some *Anthias* species are shy (especially when new to the aquarium) and may be bullied by more aggressive fishes. Should be kept only with their own kind in large groups (eight or more), and only one male should be kept.

HOW compatible with invertebrates?

Almost always safe with all invertebrates.

WHAT do they cost?

★★★☆☆   ★★★★★

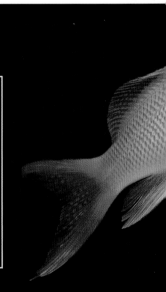

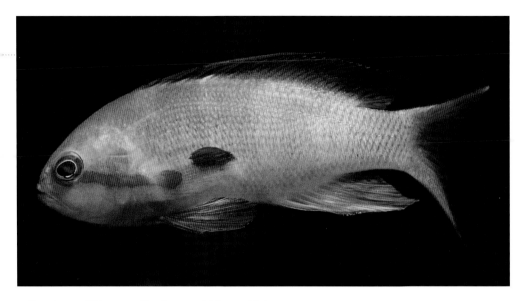

▼ Female wreckfishes are attractive but aggressive; they should be kept singly or in large groups.

▲ Male wreckfish are very different in color from females—if anything, even more attractive.

Wreckfish
Pseudanthias squamipinnis

This is the most frequently seen Pseudanthias species in the aquarium trade, and it is one of the hardier members of the family, as well as being very attractive. However, it is quite a territorial species and may attack other planktivorous fishes. It is best kept singly or in groups of at least eight females, with or without a male.

WHAT size? 6 in. (15 cm)
WHAT min size tank? 48 x 24 x 24 in. (120 x 60 x 60 cm)
WHERE is it from? Red Sea, across the Indian Ocean and western Pacific Ocean from East Africa to Niue, north to southern Japan, south to Great Barrier Reef.

Tiger queen anthias
Pseudanthias lori

This is a more subtly colored Pseudanthias than most, but it is relatively hardy. It is a deep-water species, seldom captured at depths of less than 82 ft. (25 m) and can be found as deep as 230 ft. (70 m). At the upper end of its depth range it is often found in caves and under overhangs, and it prefers less intense lighting in the aquarium.

WHAT size? 5 in. (12 cm)
WHAT min size tank? 48 x 24 x 24 in. (120 x 60 x 60 cm)
WHERE is it from? Rowley Shoals in the Indian Ocean to Tuamoto in the Pacific Ocean; ranges as far north as the Philippines, south to the Great Barrier Reef.

Anthias species

Bicolor anthias
Pseudanthias bicolor

This is one of the easiest Pseudanthias *species to keep in the aquarium, more peaceful than many others. It is a deep-water species and prefers subdued lighting, especially when first introduced into the aquarium; over time it usually adjusts to brighter conditions. Provide caves for shelter.*
WHAT size? *5 in. (13 cm)*
WHAT min size tank? *48 x 24 x 24 in. (120 x 60 x 60 cm)*
WHERE is it from? *Indian and Pacific Oceans: from Mauritius to Hawaii and Line Islands, north to Ryukyu Islands, south to Loyalty, Marshall, and Caroline Islands.*

Squareblock anthias
Pseudanthias pleurotaenia

This large Pseudanthias *species is very attractive and males are unmistakable for any other species. It should be kept singly or in groups of at least eight—but with only a single male. It needs relatively subdued lighting, as it is captured in deep water, and likes to have plenty of hiding places. It may fight with other planktivorous fishes.*

WHAT size? *8 in. (20 cm)*
WHAT min size tank? *60 x 24 x 24 in. (150 x 60 x 60 cm)*
WHERE is it from? *Pacific Ocean from Indonesia to Samoa, Ryukyu Islands to New Caledonia, also Rowley Shoals in Indian Ocean.*

Bartlett's anthias
Pseudanthias bartlettorum

One of the best Pseudanthias *species for the aquarium, but the delicate beauty of this hardy fish belies an assertive nature. Groups of females can be kept, with or without a male, but no more than one male should be kept, even in very large aquariums. It is a very active species, and needs more space than its size would suggest.*

WHAT size? *3.5 in. (9 cm)*
WHAT min size tank? *48 x 18 x 15 in. (120 x 45 x 38 cm)*
WHERE is it from? *Pacific Ocean: Palau, Caroline Islands, Marshall Islands, Kiribati, and Tonga.*

Serranocirrhitus latus

Fathead, or hawkfish, anthias

PROFILE

This species looks a lot like an anthias, but behaves very differently. Rather than swimming in open water in large shoals, it is a secretive species that lives in caves and under overhangs, alone or in small groups.

WHAT size?
5 in. (13 cm)

WHERE is it from?
Western Pacific: from Moluccas to Fiji and Tonga, north to Izu Islands, south to Great Barrier Reef and New Caledonia.

WHERE does it live in the wild?
Occurs at depths of 50–230 ft. (15–70 m), singly or in small groups, near coral reefs, particularly around ledges, drop-offs, and caves. Sometimes swims upside down close to overhangs.

WHAT aquarium environment?
Needs plenty of caves and crevices as hiding places; lots of rocks and invertebrates. Prefers relatively subdued light, especially when new to the aquarium.

WHAT minimum size tank?
48 x 18 x 15 in. (120 x 45 x 45 cm)

WHAT does it eat?
Frozen crustaceans (mysis, krill, brineshrimp, copepods) and flake foods.

HOW hardy?
Reasonably hardy provided that the aquarium environment is correct and its tankmates are suitable.

HOW compatible with other fishes?
Generally peaceful, may be bullied by more aggressive species. More than one can be kept in a large aquarium.

HOW compatible with invertebrates?
Usually safe with all invertebrates.

WHAT does it cost?
★★★★☆ ★★★★★

◀ Serranocirrhitus latus *looks like an anthias but behaves more like a gramma or forktail.*

Serranus species

Basses

PROFILE

The miniature—and in some case not so miniature—basses of the genus *Serranus* are attractive, if unusual, fishes for the reef aquarium. They come from various parts of the tropical west Atlantic, rather than the usual Indian or west Pacific Ocean sources for aquarium fishes. With the exception of the chalk bass *(Serranus tortugarum)*, they are not brightly colored but are usually attractively patterned. They are rather sedentary fishes, but are quite predatory—any shrimp or fish that will fit in their mouths is at risk.

WHERE do they live in the wild?

Usually over rubble or rocky seabed, or among corals, sometimes over sand or silty seabed. Some species in small groups, others singly or in pairs.

WHAT aquarium environment?

Some open water for swimming and caves for shelter; not highly active species so do not require very large tanks for their size.

WHAT do they eat?

Frozen meaty foods of suitable size: brineshrimp, mysis, and krill for smaller individuals, chopped squid, whole shrimp, and lancefish for larger ones.

HOW hardy?

Very hardy and disease resistant.

HOW compatible with other fishes?

Basses should not be kept with fishes they can eat—this is obviously more of a problem with the larger species. Not usually aggressive toward fishes they cannot eat. Most species can be kept with others of their own species.

HOW compatible with invertebrates?

Safe with sessile invertebrates, but will eat shrimps—again, this is more of an issue with larger species, although all basses have large mouths for their size.

WHAT do they cost?

★★☆☆☆　★★★★☆

Tobacco bass
Serranus tabacarius

This an exceptionally hardy species, but one that should not be kept with small fishes or shrimps; it has a large mouth and a predatory nature, although it is not usually territorial and fishes too large to eat will seldom be harassed by it. It can be kept in groups or pairs, but all individuals should be added to the aquarium together, and should be of similar size.

WHAT size? 9 in. (22 cm)
WHAT min size tank? 48 x 24 x 24 in. (120 x 60 x 60 cm)
WHERE is it from? Western Atlantic: southern Florida, Bahamas, and Bermuda to northern Brazil, Caribbean Sea.

Chalk bass
Serranus tortugarum

With its lovely blue coloration and very peaceful nature, this is probably the best Serranus bass for the aquarium. It can be kept in small groups (all should be added to the aquarium at the same time). Only the smallest of shrimps are at risk from this species. It is best kept with quiet tankmates, as it may be bullied by more aggressive fishes.

WHAT size? *3 in. (8 cm)*
WHAT min size tank? *36 x 15 x 12 in. (90 x 38 x 30 cm)*
WHERE is it from? *Western Atlantic: southern Florida, Bahamas, Honduras, and Virgin Islands.*

Harlequin bass
Serranus tigrinus

Less often kept than some of its relatives. This is quite a hefty species, and a predatory one, so should not be kept with shrimps or small fishes. It can be kept in pairs in large aquariums. Other large, assertive fishes make ideal tank companions.

WHAT size? *11.5 in. (29 cm)*
WHAT min size tank? *60 x 24 x 24 in. (150 x 60 x 60 cm)*
WHERE is it from? *Western Atlantic: southern Florida, Bermuda to northern South America, Caribbean Sea.*

The harlequin bass looks predatory—and is!

Gramma species

Grammas

The grammas are a small family of very brightly colored little fishes that come from the tropical west Atlantic. They are ideal fishes for reef aquariums that are densely packed with live rock, as this nicely represents their natural habitat. They like to stay close to cover and will usually identify a cave or overhang and adopt it as a home—defending it fiercely against other fishes. They will sometimes hover upside down under overhangs. The royal gramma *(Gramma loreto)* and blackcap gramma *(G. melacara)* have been reported to spawn in captivity. Males are reported to tend nests containing the eggs.

WHERE do they live in the wild?
Usually found on steep reef walls and drop-offs, close to caves and crevices, typically with their bellies aligned to the substrate.

WHAT aquarium environment?
Prefer subdued lighting and plenty of rocks and invertebrates to provide caves and overhangs.

WHAT do they eat?
Need a mixed diet of frozen crustaceans and high-quality flake foods. Feed at least once daily.

HOW hardy?
Usually very robust in the aquarium. Colors may fade if they do not receive a good, varied diet.

HOW compatible with other fishes?
Will fiercely defend their chosen territory (usually a hole or cave), but are generally peaceful and may be bullied by more aggressive fishes. Some species can be kept in groups.

HOW compatible with invertebrates?
Only the very smallest shrimps are at risk from grammas. Sessile invertebrates will be ignored.

WHAT do they cost?
★★★☆☆ ★★★★★

Royal gramma
Gramma loreto

This is a stunningly beautiful species, and easy to keep provided the aquarium environment is appropriate. It can be kept in groups in larger tanks. It can be distinguished from the similar-looking false gramma (Pictichromis paccagnellae) by the dark bar through the eye (absent in the false gramma), and the fact that the meeting of the yellow and magenta colors is not as sharp—yellow scales overlap into the magenta forepart of the body—in the royal gramma.

WHAT size? *3 in. (8 cm)*
WHAT min size tank? *36 x 15 x 12 in. (90 x 38 x 30 cm)*
WHERE is it from? *Western central Atlantic: Bahamas, Bermuda, and Central America to northern South America.*

Blackcap gramma
Gramma melacara

Slightly larger and more aggressive in nature than the royal gramma, the blackcap gramma is a species from deep water and prefers subdued lighting. Although it can ultimately become very territorial, it is often shy when first added to the aquarium, especially if large or active fishes are already present.

WHAT size? *4 in. (10 cm)*
WHAT min size tank? *36 x 18 x 15 in. (90 x 45 x 38 cm)*
WHERE is it from? *Western central Atlantic: West Indies, including Bahamas and Central America.*

Assessor species

Forktails

PROFILE

There are three species of *Assessor*, usually known as forktails or sometimes devilfishes. Two of the three species are imported for the aquarium trade—the third, *A. randalli*, is little known, even to marine biologists. The yellow and blue forktails are highly desirable aquarium fishes, especially for smaller tanks and nano-reef aquariums, although they can sometimes be expensive, as they come from Australia's Great Barrier Reef.

WHERE do they live in the wild?

Live in groups in caves and crevices on coral reefs, often swimming upside-down under overhangs and cave roofs. Usually found in relatively shallow water.

WHAT aquarium environment?

Plenty of rocks and invertebrates, preferably with caves and overhangs. No particular requirements with respect to lighting.

WHAT do they eat?

Frozen crustaceans of suitable size (copepods, brineshrimp, mysis), frozen fish and lobster roe, flake food and small pellets. Should be fed at least twice daily.

HOW hardy?

Very hardy and disease resistant.

HOW compatible with other fishes?

Peaceful with other fishes and may be bullied by more aggressive species. Ideally should be kept with quiet tankmates. Can be kept in pairs or small groups: all individuals should be added at the same time. Males are usually larger than females, so groups should contain one larger fish and several smaller individuals.

HOW compatible with invertebrates?

Harmless to all invertebrates.

WHAT do they cost?

★★★☆☆　★★★★★

Yellow forktail
Assessor flavissimus

A wonderful fish for any aquarium with suitably quiet, nonaggressive tankmates that are not large enough to eat it. It often swims upside-down under overhangs. This is a particularly good species for nano-reef aquariums.

WHAT size? *2 in. (5 cm)*
WHAT min size tank? *24 x 12 x 12 in. (60 x 30 x 30 cm)*
WHERE is it from? *Great Barrier Reef, Queensland, Australia.*

Blue forktail
Assessor macneilli

The deep indigo color of this species is almost unique among marine fishes. Like the yellow forktail, it is a perfect nano-reef aquarium fish when kept singly, although groups need larger tanks.

WHAT size? *2.4 in. (6 cm)*
WHAT min size tank? *24 x 12 x 12 in. (60 x 30 x 30 cm)*
WHERE is it from? *Western Pacific Ocean: Great Barrier Reef, Queensland, Australia, and New Caledonia.*

Pseudochromis and *Pictichromis* species

Dottybacks

The often astonishingly brightly colored dottybacks are mainly small fishes that live close to rock and coral substrates, hunting small invertebrates. There are some larger species, but these are usually extremely territorial, to the point where they pose a severe danger to most tankmates. Many of the smaller species are also very territorial, particularly the *Pictichromis* species. Although until recently included in the genus *Pseudochromis*, these species are morphologically different from the true *Pseudochromis* species, as typified by *P. fridmani*, the orchid dottyback. The latter are long, slender fishes, usually with long, flowing fins, and (although there are exceptions) are among the less aggressive dottybacks. The *Pictichromis* species, in contrast, have shorter, stockier bodies, less flamboyant fins— and tend to be much more aggressive. Several species have been tank-bred on a commercial scale.

WHERE do they live in the wild?
Typically found among branching corals or coral rubble, ranging from shallow water to around 230 ft. (70 m) depth, depending on species. Some species occur in dense populations, with several individuals per square yard.

WHAT aquarium environment?
Prefer aquariums with plenty of rocks and invertebrates, with many caves and crevices.

WHAT do they eat?
Frozen crustaceans and fish roe, dried foods. Feed at least twice daily. Also hunt small creatures (particularly bristleworms).

HOW hardy?
Generally very hardy.

HOW compatible with other fishes?
Most *Pseudochromis* species are generally peaceful with unrelated fishes, and in reasonably large tanks many species can be kept as groups or with other peaceful *Pseudochromis*. *Pictichromis* species tend to be highly territorial and should be kept only with robust tankmates.

HOW compatible with invertebrates?
Pseudochromis species are usually safe with all invertebrates. *Pictichromis* dottybacks leave sessile invertebrates alone, but may attack and kill (but often not eat) shrimps, including *Lysmata* cleaner shrimps.

WHAT do they cost?
★☆☆☆   ★★★★☆

Sunrise dottyback
Pseudochromis flavivertex

This species is rather stockier than many other Pseudochromis *species. It is fairly peaceful in the aquarium, if anything being rather shy when kept with more active species. Its colors are prone to fading if it is not fed a good diet.*

WHAT size? *3 in. (7 cm)*
WHAT min size tank? *30 x 15 x 12 in. (75 x 38 x 30)*
WHERE is it from? *Red Sea and Gulf of Aden.*

▽

Orchid dottyback
Pseudochromis fridmani

If there is a perfect marine aquarium fish, this is it: small enough to keep in anything from a nano-reef tank upward; peaceful and completely safe with invertebrates. It can be bred in the aquarium, is easy to feed, hardy— and very beautiful. Its only downside is a high price in both wild-caught and tank-bred form.

WHAT size? *2.5 in. (6 cm)*
WHAT min size tank? *24 x 15 x 12 in. (60 x 38 x 30 cm)*
WHERE is it from? *Red Sea.*

Sankey's dottyback
Pseudochromis sankeyi

Distinctively colored with its black and white stripes, this species is also one of the more peaceful dottybacks. In larger aquariums it can be kept in small groups, and will mix with other peaceful Pseudochromis *species, such as P. fridmani and P. springeri. However, it should not be kept with its own or related species in small tanks.*

WHAT size? *3 in. (7 cm)*
WHAT min size tank? *30 x 15 x 12 in. (75 x 38 x 30 cm)*
WHERE is it from? *Red Sea and Gulf of Aden.*

Dottybacks

Springer's dottyback
Pseudochromis springeri

An unmistakable species, with its velvety black body and neon stripes on the head, this very small dottyback is an excellent choice for the nano-reef aquarium. Despite its small size it can be quite territorial, especially in smaller aquariums, although it will live with other dottybacks, especially the more peaceful ones, in medium to large tanks.

WHAT size? *2 in. (5 cm)*
WHAT min size tank? *24 x 12 x 12 in. (60 x 30 x 30 cm)*
WHERE is it from? *Red Sea.*

Neon dottyback
Pseudochromis aldabraensis

This species and the very similar P. dutoiti are exceptions to the general rule that the slender Pseudochromis species are not highly aggressive—it should not be kept with smaller fishes or less assertive ones. A community of larger fishes, particularly quite tough ones, is a better bet for this belligerent species.

WHAT size? *4 in. (10 cm)*
WHAT min size tank? *48 x 18 x 15 in. (120 x 45 x 38 cm)*
WHERE is it from? *Indian Ocean: from Aldabra and Persian Gulf, Gulf of Oman, coast of Pakistan, and Sri Lanka.*

Diadem dottyback
Pictichromis diadema

This is a dazzling little fish, but a territorial one. Small groups can be kept in very large reef aquariums with plenty of live rock, but in general it is best housed with larger tankmates. It needs a good, vitamin-rich diet to maintain its vivid colors in the long term.

WHAT size? *2.5 in. (6 cm)*
WHAT min size tank? *24 x 15 x 12 in. (60 x 38 x 30 cm)*
WHERE is it from? *Western central Pacific Ocean: Malaysia to western Philippines.*

False gramma
Pictichromis paccagnellae

A very beautiful, but highly aggressive little dottyback, this species will fight even with much larger fishes. It needs a vitamin-rich diet to maintain its dazzling colors. It makes a good species to keep on its own in a nano-reef aquarium.

WHAT size? *3 in. (7 cm)*
WHAT min size tank? *30 x 15 x 12 in. (75 x 38 x 30 cm)*
WHERE is it from? *Western Pacific Ocean: Indonesia to Vanuatu, including Palau.*

Strawberry dottyback
Pictichromis porphyreus

Superficially similar to Pseudochromis fridmani, *this species, although less expensive, is less desirable in most reef aquarium situations because it is much more aggressive. It can be distinguished from P. fridmani by the lack of a dark bar through the eye, a stockier, less elongated build, and the fact that its fins are not solidly colored magenta like those of P. fridmani but are usually clear. It makes a better inhabitant for a tank with larger, more aggressive tankmates than P. fridmani does.*

WHAT size? *2.5 in. (6 cm)*
WHAT min size tank? *24 x 15 x 12 in. (60 x 38 x 30 cm)*
WHERE is it from? *Western Pacific Ocean: the Philippines to Samoa, north to southern Japan, south to Admiralty Islands.*

Wrasses

▶ The wrasses (Labridae) are one of the larger fish families, with well over 600 known species—and more being discovered all the time. Wrasses can be found throughout the world's oceans, and range in size from around 2 in. (5 cm) (the tiny possum wrasses, *Wetmorella* species) to 6.5 ft. (2 m) behemoths, such as the humphead, or Napoleon wrasse *(Cheilinus undulatus)*. One feature many wrasses share is being very colorful. The tropical members of the family take this to extremes in some cases—many are among the most colorful fishes that can be kept in the aquarium. Many of the best wrasses for the reef aquarium belong to a few genera, and within a genus the aquarium husbandry required is often similar between species. However, a few species do not fit into these categories. The fish profiles presented here reflect this.

Price guide

★	$24–32
★★	$32–48
★★★	$48–80
★★★★	$96–120
★★★★★	$128–192

PROFILE

The fairy wrasses (*Cirrhilabrus* species) include some of the most dazzling fishes for the reef aquarium, many having astonishingly bright colors and patterns. They can change their colors very rapidly according to mood, and males of some species show great variation in appearance between geographical areas. Males typically also intensify their colors when courting females. They are more than beautiful, however; they are near-perfect aquarium inhabitants. Most are bold fishes that swim high in the water column looking for plankton. Males and females often look very different (males are generally more colorful), and it is possible to keep a male with a group of females.

Their only weakness is a propensity to jump from open tanks, so you should keep the aquarium well covered.

WHERE do they live in the wild?

Usually found around reef margins or rubble slopes, typically in habitats, at depths ranging from one to 3 to 330 ft. (100 m), depending on the species, although most are found in relatively shallow water. They live in small or large schools, sometimes of mixed species, sometimes

Fairy wrasses

including other planktivorous fishes. They swim fairly close to the substrate, and at night sleep in crevices.

WHAT aquarium environment?

Plenty of open water plus some caves and crevices for shelter. Some deep-water species prefer subdued illumination, but most of those featured here have no preferences with respect to lighting.

WHAT do they eat?

Accept most frozen and dried foods of suitable size; frozen crustaceans (mysis, brineshrimp, krill, copepods) and fish and lobster roe are ideal. Should be fed at least twice daily.

HOW hardy?

Generally hardy and easy to keep; the only major threat is jumping out of the aquarium.

HOW compatible with other fishes?

Females can be kept in groups with or without a male, but only one male of a species should be kept per tank. Males of different species can usually be kept together, provided they are dissimilar in appearance. Generally ignore unrelated fishes, but occasionally chase smaller planktivorous species.

Any territoriality is usually reduced in larger aquariums.

HOW compatible with invertebrates?

Almost always safe with all invertebrates. Will not bother corals or clams, and only very small shrimps may be at risk from larger fairy wrasses.

WHAT do they cost?

★☆☆☆☆ ★★★★★
C. lubbocki is the least expensive (★) and C. jordani the most expensive (★★★★★).

▼ *This male Scott's wrasse,* Cirrhilabrus scottorum, *shows just how beautiful these fishes can be.*

Cirrhilabrus species

Fairy wrasses

Goldflash fairy wrasse
Cirrhilabrus aurantidorsalis

This very attractive wrasse is being imported more frequently than before. It is a very extroverted fish, usually out on display, often swimming close to the water surface.

WHAT size? *3.5 in. (9 cm)*
WHAT min size tank? *36 x 18 x 18 in. (90 x 45 x 45 cm)*
WHERE is it from? *Western central Pacific Ocean.*

Exquisite fairy wrasse
Cirrhilabrus exquisitus

Males of this species look spectacular when displaying to females or other males, flashing different patterns rapidly. Two forms of this fish are sold, usually as the "exquisite wrasse" (from the Indian Ocean) and the "Pacific exquisite wrasse." Both are probably the same species.

WHAT size? *4.5 in. (11 cm)*
WHAT min size tank? *48 x 18 x 18 in. (120 x 45 x 45 cm)*
WHERE is it from? *Indian Ocean, east to Sumatra.*

◁ Flame fairy wrasse
Cirrhilabrus jordani

The flame fairy wrasse, a stunningly colored, deep-water fish from Hawaii, commands a high price. Both males and females are very colorful. Lower light levels are better for this species, at least initially. It is a very hardy species.

WHAT size? *4 in. (10 cm)*
WHAT min size tank? *48 x 18 x 18 in. (120 x 45 x 45 cm)*
WHERE is it from? *Hawaii.*

Laboute's fairy wrasse
Cirrhilabrus laboutei

The color pattern of this species is so distinctive as to make it unmistakable for any other fish. Juveniles and adults, males and females all look similar, although mature males tend to have more intense colors.

WHAT size? *3 in. (7.5 cm)*
WHAT min size tank? *36 x 18 x 15 in. (90 x 45 x 38 cm)*
WHERE is it from? *Western Pacific: Great Barrier Reef and New Caledonia.*

▽

73

Fairy wrasses

◁ Ruby head fairy wrasse
Cirrhilabrus rubrisquamis

This lovely species tends to stay closer to the substrate than some other fairy wrasses, swimming among invertebrates and through rockwork, rather than cruising in open water. It is less assertive than some of its relatives.

WHAT size? *3 in. (7.5 cm)*
WHAT min size tank? *36 x 18 x 15 in. (90 x 45 x 38 cm)*
WHERE is it from? *Western Indian Ocean.*

Yellowstreak fairy wrasse
Cirrhilabrus luteovittatus

Males of this species are very spectacular, with beautiful, intricate color patterns in their fins. This is a close relative of the koi fairy wrasse (C. solorensis); juveniles of the two species are almost identical. It is found in deeper water and prefers less brightly lit conditions, especially when new to the aquarium.

WHAT size? *4 in. (10 cm)*
WHAT min size tank? *48 x 18 x 15 in. (120 x 45 x 38 cm)*
WHERE is it from? *Western Pacific: eastern Micronesia.*

Yellow blotch fairy wrasse
Cirrhilabrus lyukyuensis

Sometimes considered to be a variant of another species—the blueheaded fairy wrasse (C. cyanopleura)—this is a beautiful and very hardy species, as well as being one of the largest fairy wrasses. Females can look quite similar to males.

WHAT size? *6 in. (15 cm)*
WHAT min size tank? *60 x 24 x 18 in. (150 x 60 x 45 cm)*
WHERE is it from? *Wide range from eastern Indian Ocean to western Pacific, including Andaman Sea, Indonesia, Christmas Island, the Philippines, Great Barrier Reef, Palau, Papua New Guinea, Ryukyu Islands, and Taiwan.*

Lubbock's fairy wrasse
Cirrhilabrus lubbocki

This is one of the most variable in color of all fairy wrasses. It is usually inexpensive and readily available, and a very hardy fish in the aquarium.

WHAT size? *3.5 in. (9 cm)*
WHAT min size tank? *36 x 18 x 15 in. (90 x 45 x 38 cm)*
WHERE is it from? *Western central Pacific, Philippines to Celebes.*

Cirrhilabrus species

Fairy wrasses

Sea fighter or long-finned fairy wrasse
Cirrhilabrus rubriventralis

Also known as the long-finned fairy wrasse, this is one of the most popular and least expensive Cirrhilabrus *species. It is usually a very peaceful fish. Like others in the family it can change color rapidly.*

What size? *3 in. (7.5 cm)*
What minimum tank size? *36 x 18 x 15 in. (90 x 45 x 38 cm)*
Where is it from? *Western Indian Ocean, Red Sea.*

Redmargin fairy wrasse
Cirrhilabrus rubromarginatus

This is a deep-water fairy wrasse that tends to be expensive and not always easy to find. It prefers relatively low light levels, so is not a fish for brightly lit Acropora aquariums.

WHAT size? *5 in. (12 cm)*
WHAT min size tank? *48 x 24 x 18 in. (120 x 60 x 45 cm)*
WHERE is it from? *Western Pacific, from Vanuatu, Fiji, and Tonga to Indonesia and north to Ryukyu Islands.*

Scott's fairy wrasse
Cirrhilabrus scottorum

Males of this species are stunningly beautiful, but extremely variable in color and pattern, depending on where they were collected, as well as on their mood. It is one of the larger and more aggressive fairy wrasses.

WHAT size? *5 in. (12 cm)*
WHAT min size tank? *48 x 18 x 18 in . (120 x 45 x 45 cm)*
WHERE is it from? *South Pacific Ocean, from the Great Barrier Reef to the Pitcairn Islands.*

Koi fairy wrasse
Cirrhilabrus solorensis

This species is highly variable in color: some males are turquoise to almost green on the flanks, others blue— it is thought that these represent populations from different areas. Females look quite similar to the goldflash fairy wrasse (C. aurantidorsalis).

WHAT size? *4 in. (10 cm)*
WHAT min size tank? *48 x 18 x 15 in. (120 x 45 x 38 cm)*
WHERE is it from? *Western central Pacific Ocean.*

Halichoeres wrasses

PROFILE

Halichoeres is one of the larger genera of wrasses, with 76 current valid species. Different *Halichoeres* wrasses are found in most tropical seas. They include many small, colorful species that are well suited to the general reef aquarium, as well as some larger fishes that make good inhabitants for bigger or more specialized tanks. In addition to the species described here, many others appear in the aquarium trade, although often infrequently and sometimes without proper identification,

Many species live in groups in the wild, and in some cases these appear to be haremic, with a male fish associating with several females. In the aquarium, keeping two or more young fishes together may result in a dominant individual becoming male, a process usually accompanied by alterations in color or pattern, although these changes may be quite subtle.

WHERE do they live in the wild?

Found in a wide range of environments, including coral reefs, seagrass beds, estuaries, sand flats, and harbors. They are always found in areas with sand or rubble beds, as at night they sleep buried in the substrate. Many species live in shallow water, but some have been found at depths of up to 280 ft. (85 m). They live in loose aggregations, sometimes of mixed species. They usually swim close to the substrate.

WHAT aquarium environment?

Must have a bed of fine sand in which to sleep or hide. Plenty of live rock is beneficial to provide opportunities for hunting. No preferences with respect to lighting.

WHAT do they eat?

Accept most frozen and dried foods of suitable size. Should be fed at least once daily.

HOW hardy?

Generally hardy and easy to keep. Some species appear to be extremely disease resistant.

Silver-belly wrasse
Halichoeres leucoxanthus

This little wrasse is very resistant to parasitic infections. It can be kept in groups, where one fish will usually become a male, which is signaled by the development of green markings on the face, a slight hump on the head, and a change in the shade of yellow on the body.

WHAT size? *5 in. (12 cm)*
WHAT min size tank? *48 x 18 x 18 in. (120 x 45 x 45 cm)*
WHERE is it from? *Western Indian Ocean, east to Java.*

HOW compatible with other fishes?

Most *Halichoeres* wrasses are reasonably peaceful toward unrelated tankmates (although there are occasional exceptions). Some species can be kept in groups.

HOW compatible with invertebrates?

The *Halichoeres* wrasses described here are usually completely harmless to sessile invertebrates, and will generally leave all other invertebrates stocked by the fishkeeper alone, although larger individuals may sometimes eat very small shrimps. However, these wrasses can have a major impact on the microfauna of the aquarium—the tiny worms, snails, crustaceans,

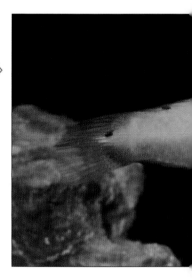

and so on that come into the tank with live rock and often build up substantial populations. In some cases this is useful (where the wrasse is eating pest flatworms, for example), but generally the victims of predation are beneficial creatures, such as bristleworms and amphipods. This does not seem to have major adverse effects on the aquarium system, but fishes such as mandarins and scooters (*Synchiropus* species) that rely on the microfauna as their food can suffer if kept in the same tank as *Halichoeres* species.

WHAT do they cost?
★☆☆☆☆   ★★☆☆☆

Banana wrasse
Halichoeres chrysus

This is a lovely all-yellow fish that is perfect for a medium-sized reef tank, where it can be kept in a small group. It is an extremely hardy species that is usually peaceful towards its tankmates.

WHAT size? *4 in. (10 cm)*
WHAT min size tank? *48 x 18 x 15 in. (120 x 45 x 38 cm)*
WHERE is it from? *Widespread from Indian Ocean to west Pacific, Christmas Island to Bali.*

Halichoeres wrasses

Radiant wrasse
Halichoeres iridis

▷

The radiant wrasse has an unmistakable color scheme, very unusual in fishes, being darker on the flanks and belly than on the back, where the pale yellow color seems to give the fish a glowing outline— hence the common name.

WHAT size? *4.5 in. (11 cm)*
WHAT min size tank? *48 x 18 x 15 in. (120 x 45 x 38 cm)*
WHERE is it from? *Red Sea and western Indian Ocean.*

◁ ## Green wrasse
Halichoeres chloropterus

A fish for the larger reef tank. When full grown, this species is likely to eat ornamental shrimps. Plain bright green as a juvenile (as here), it typically develops a dark blotch and rows of tiny black spots on the flanks as it matures, and large males develop pink markings on the head and front half of the body.

WHAT size? *7 in. (18 cm)*
WHAT min size tank? *60 x 24 x 18 in. (150 x 60 x 45 cm)*
WHERE is it from? *Western central Pacific from the Philippines to Great Barrier Reef.*

◁ **Pinstripe wrasse**
Halichoeres melanurus

This wrasse is very widespread in the western Pacific; local populations show some variations in color, and it can be difficult to differentiate this fish from a number of similar species. It is a useful predator of several "pest" invertebrates.

WHAT size? *5 in. (12 cm)*
WHAT min size tank? *48 x 18 x 18 in. (120 x 45 x 45 cm)*
WHERE is it from? *Western Pacific from Japan to Great Barrier Reef, Samoa, and Tonga.*

Ornate wrasse ▷
Halichoeres ornatissimus

Many Halichoeres wrasses have very intricate patterns, and it can be difficult to tell the species apart, particularly as even within a species there can be wide variation in coloration between juveniles and adults, males and females, and populations from different areas.

WHAT size? *7 in. (18 cm)*
WHAT min size tank? *60 x 24 x 18 in. (150 x 60 x 45 cm)*
WHERE is it from? *Wide range from Indian Ocean to Hawaii, Japan to Great Barrier Reef.*

Bodianus bimaculatus

Candy hogfish

PROFILE

The candy hogfish *(Bodianus bimaculatus)*, also known as the twinspot hogfish (a translation of its scientific name), is a stunningly attractive little wrasse, with some unusual colors for a marine fish. The basic hue is bright yellow, but on the back this shades into a metallic gold, a color more often seen on a koi than a wrasse. Along the flanks is a streak of pale pink, an equally rare color in a saltwater fish.

Once settled into the aquarium, this is a very bold species that is almost constantly on view, cruising in midwater or over the surfaces of rocks and sand looking for small prey.

WHAT size?
4 in. (10 cm)

WHERE is it from?
Indian and Pacific Oceans, from Madagascar to New Caledonia, Japan to New Zealand.

WHERE does it live in the wild?
Found on sandy slopes, outer reef slopes, and among rubble, most commonly at depths of greater than 130 ft. (40 m). It tends to live in small aggregations, sometimes with other wrasses.

WHAT aquarium environment?
A balance of plenty of open water and lots of live rock to provide hunting opportunities. Although often found in relatively deep water, it adapts readily to aquariums with bright lighting.

WHAT minimum size tank?
48 x 18 x 15 in. (120 x 45 x 38 cm)

WHAT does it eat?
Feeds readily on most frozen and dry foods. Should be fed at least once daily.

HOW hardy?
Like other hogfishes, this is a robust, hardy species. It is not particularly susceptible to disease, but is prone to jumping from open aquariums.

HOW compatible with other fishes?
Small juveniles are generally peaceful toward most other fishes, but become bolder and sometimes more territorial with increasing size. The most likely

▼ *This colorful species is one of the few hogfishes suitable for a typical reef aquarium.*

targets for aggression are smaller or more docile wrasses, such as flasher wrasses (*Paracheilinus* species) and the smaller and less assertive of the fairy wrasses (*Cirrhilabrus* species). Do not keep it with others of its own species.

HOW compatible with invertebrates?
Harmless to almost all invertebrates: no threat to corals or clams, and only the smallest of shrimps are at risk of being eaten—and only by the largest candy hogfishes.

WHAT does it cost?
★★☆☆☆   ★★★☆☆

BODIANUS WRASSES

The *Bodianus* wrasses, commonly known as hogfishes, are generally quite large fishes that are too predatory and active for most reef tanks. However, there are two smaller members of the family that can be kept in the reef aquarium, provided that their tankmates are suitable.

Bodianus species

Candycane hogfish

PROFILE

This beautiful species, also known as the Pacific redstriped hogfish, is currently lacking a full scientific name. It is found in deep water, so tends to be rather expensive. In the aquarium, the candycane hogfish is an extroverted species, almost always out on view.

There are some similarly colored species, such as *B. opercularis* (which grows to 7 in. [18 cm] and comes from the Red Sea and Indian Ocean), and *B. masudai* (a 5-in. [12-cm] species from Japan, Norfolk Island, and New Caledonia), but these are much less common in the aquarium trade. The candycane hogfish can be distinguished from both these species by their lack of a black spot on the caudal peduncle. Also, although *B. opercularis* has a similar build to the candycane hogfish, *B. masudai* is a stouter fish. The care required for these other species is probably similar to that required for the candycane hogfish, but there is much less aquarium experience with them.

WHAT size?
4 in. (10 cm)

WHERE is it from?
West, central, and south Pacific Ocean.

WHERE does it live in the wild?
Lives in deep water, 66–200 ft. (20–60 m) or more, in reef walls. It has been observed living in small groups.

WHAT aquarium environment?
Likes plenty of open water for swimming but also plenty of live rock. Adapts readily to aquariums with bright lighting, despite its deep-water origins.

WHAT minimum size tank?
48 x 18 x 15 in. (120 x 45 x 38 cm)

WHAT does it eat?
Will eat most frozen and dry foods. Should be fed at least once daily.

HOW hardy?
A robust, hardy species, with no particular susceptibility to disease. The main threat to this species is jumping from an uncovered aquarium.

▲ *The candycane hogfish is one of several similarly colored species. Hardy and adaptable.*

HOW compatible with other fishes?
Small individuals are usually peaceful toward fish tankmates, but larger ones are more territorial, particularly toward similarly shaped wrasses. Do not keep this species with others of its own kind.

HOW compatible with invertebrates?
Usually poses no threat to invertebrates, but one case of a large individual attacking a recently moulted boxing shrimp *(Stenopus hispidus)* has been reported.

WHAT does it cost?
★★★☆☆

Paracheilinus species

Flasher wrasses

PROFILE

Flasher wrasses are very colorful small planktivores that make ideal inhabitants for the reef aquarium, particularly as members of a peaceful fish community. They owe their name to the displays of male fishes when courting females or engaging in territorial disputes with other males. The males rapidly flare their large dorsal and anal fins, providing a sudden flash of vivid color. In the aquarium, they spend most of their time swimming in midwater, provided that no aggressive planktivores are present.

WHERE do they live in the wild?

Found over rocky areas and coral reefs, feeding on zooplankton. They generally stay close to the seabed. Most species are found at depths of 6–130 ft. (15–40 m), although some are found in deeper water. The females and juveniles of most species live in mixed-species aggregations, whereas males are found in groups of their own species. At night they sleep in crevices in rocks, in mucus cocoons, which are thought to prevent nocturnal predators from locating them.

WHAT aquarium environment?

Plenty of open water for swimming, as well as extensive areas of live rock to provide hiding places. No major preferences with respect to lighting.

WHAT do they eat?

Readily accept most small frozen foods, especially when presented in midwater. Copepods, brineshrimp, fish and lobster roe are ideal. Will usually adapt to eating dried foods. Should be fed at least twice daily.

HOW hardy?

Generally hardy and easy to keep. May jump from open aquariums.

HOW compatible with other fishes?

Peaceful toward most tankmates, with the exception of related species, especially in smaller tanks. They can be kept in groups of several females or several females with one male in larger tanks; introduce all individuals to the tank at the same time, or add the male after the females. Other fish tankmates should be peaceful species; larger or more boisterous planktivores, such as many fairy wrasses, anthias, and *Genicanthus* angels, may intimidate flasher wrasses.

HOW compatible with invertebrates?

Flasher wrasses pose no threat to invertebrates.

WHAT do they cost?

★★☆☆☆

McCosker's flasher wrasse
Paracheilinus mccoskeri

Although one of the smallest flasher wrasses, this is still a very attractive species. It looks similar to some other species, but the base color on the body is usually more yellow than that of other flasher wrasses.

WHAT size? *2.5 in. (6.5 cm)*
WHAT min size tank? *36 x 18 x 15 in. (90 x 45 x 38 cm)*
WHERE is it from? *Western Indian Ocean to Fiji.*

Lyretail flasher wrasse
Paracheilinus angulatus

This beautiful species can be easily distinguished from most other flasher wrasses by its lyre-shaped tail fin— most other species have rounded tail fins. In the wild, it sometimes hybridizes with other Paracheilinus *species, and the resulting offspring also often have lyre-shaped tails, indicating the identity of one parent.*

WHAT size? *3 in. (7.5 cm)*
WHAT min size tank? *36 x 18 x 15 in. (90 x 45 x 38 cm)*
WHERE is it from? *Western central Pacific: the Philippines and northern Indonesia.*

Redfin flasher wrasse
Paracheilinus carpenteri

A wonderful fish for a reef tank with quiet fishes. Males are similar in color and pattern to males of the smaller P. mccoskeri and the larger P. flavianalis.

WHAT size? *3 in. (7.5 cm)*
WHAT min size tank? *36 x 18 x 15 in. (90 x 45 x 38 cm)*
WHERE is it from? *Western Pacific: Taiwan, the Philippines, to northern Indonesia.*

Blue flasher wrasse
Paracheilinus cyaneus

Males of this species are very distinctive, with shimmering metallic blue along the back and in the large dorsal fin, which is edged by long filaments that are usually red, but may also be blue.

WHAT size? *3 in. (7 cm)*
WHAT min size tank? *36 x 18 x 15 in. (90 x 45 x 38 cm)*
WHERE is it from? *Western central Pacific: Indonesia.*

Pajama wrasses and their relatives

PROFILE

Pseudocheilinus wrasses are rather shy, secretive fishes that live in complex environments with plenty of cover: among branching corals in shallow water or among caves and rubble in deeper areas. Most are very attractively colored. They are also very interesting to observe in the aquarium, as they cruise close to rocks and sand substrates, with their eyes swiveling independently of each other, scanning surfaces for small prey.

Some *Pseudocheilinus* wrasses, especially the pajama wrasse *(P. hexataenia)*, are readily available in the aquarium trade and inexpensive, but others, notably the mystery wrasse *(P. ocellatus),* are less commonly imported and can be very expensive. These wrasses can be very useful in the reef aquarium, because they are predators of a variety of "pest" invertebrates, including flatworms and small parasitic snails.

WHERE do they live in the wild?

Varies between species; Those living in shallow water are typically found among branching corals, sometimes on reef flats. Deep-water species are found among rubble at the base of reefs, and under overhangs and in caves.

WHAT aquarium environment?

Prefer extensive areas of live rock with many caves and crevices. No preferences with respect to lighting—the deep-water species usually adapt well to brightly lit tanks, although all *Pseudocheilinus* wrasses tend to spend their early days in the aquarium lurking among the rocks.

WHAT do they eat?

Will usually eat any foods offered, whether frozen or dry, provided they are of suitable size. Should be fed at least once daily.

HOW hardy?

Generally hardy and easy to keep.

Pajama wrasse
Pseudocheilinus hexataenia

The pajama wrasse, an old favorite reef aquarium fish, has a color scheme that includes almost every color of the rainbow. Despite its small size, it is quite an aggressive species that will sometimes attack fishes larger than itself.

WHAT size? *3 in. (8 cm)*
WHAT min size tank? *30 x 15 x 12 in. (75 x 38 x 30 cm)*
WHERE is it from? *Wide range from Red Sea, across Indian Ocean, Pacific as far east as Tuamoto Islands, north to Japan, south to Lord Howe and Austral Islands.*

HOW compatible with other fishes?

Most *Pseudocheilinus* species can be aggressive toward fish tankmates, particularly other wrasses—sometimes including those larger than themselves. Fishes kept with *Pseudocheilinus* species therefore need to be quite robust, and preferably bigger than the wrasse. This is particularly the case for the eight-line wrasse *(P. octotaenia).*

HOW compatible with invertebrates?

These wrasses pose no threat to sessile invertebrates. Larger individuals of most species may eat very small shrimps. *P. octotaenia* is likely to eat typical reef aquarium shrimps such as *Lysmata* species cleaner shrimps. *Pseudocheilinus* wrasses may consume many of the tiny worms,

snails, crustaceans, and so on that come from the live rock, but also eat a variety of small invertebrate pests.

WHAT do they cost?
★☆☆☆☆ ★★★★★

P. hexataenia is the least expensive (★) and *P. ocellatus* the most expensive (★★★★★).

△

Mystery wrasse
Pseudocheilinus ocellatus

This absolutely stunning species is the most expensive of the Pseudocheilinus *wrasses, but it is a hardy fish and one of the most peaceful of its family, so well worth the initial investment.*

WHAT size? 7.5 in. (19 cm)
WHAT min size tank? 36 x 18 x 15 in. (90 x 45 x 38 cm)
WHERE is it from? Western central Pacific Ocean.

△

Eight-line wrasse
Pseudocheilinus octotaenia

The largest of the Pseudocheilinus *wrasses (here a juvenile), this species is very distinctive with its pattern of orange blotches overlaid by darker stripes. It is an aggressive species and should not be kept with smaller or less assertive fishes.*

WHAT size? 5 in. (12 cm)
WHAT min size tank? 40 x 18 x 18 in. (100 x 45 x 45 cm)
WHERE is it from? Wide range across the Indian and Pacific Oceans, from East Africa to Hawaii.

Four-line wrasse
Pseudocheilinus tetrataenia

This small wrasse is beautifully colored, but best appreciated in a small aquarium where it is possible to observe it closely. It is quite territorial, particularly in small tanks, so needs robust companions.

WHAT size? 3 in. (7 cm)
WHAT min size tank? 30 x 15 x 12 in. (75 x 38 x 30 cm)
WHERE is it from? Widely distributed in the Pacific Ocean, from Japan to Hawaii and the Tuamoto Islands, as far south as the Austral Islands.

Choerodon fasciatus

Harlequin tuskfish

Large wrasses generally do not make particularly good reef aquarium fishes; although they will usually not damage corals deliberately, they tend to be highly active and predatory on most mobile invertebrates. The harlequin tuskfish is something of an exception, although it should still be added to a reef tank with caution—and with carefully chosen tankmates. This species is spectacularly colorful, right down to its prominent blue teeth. In contrast to many larger wrasses it is quite a sedate species, with younger individuals tending toward shyness.

WHAT size?
12 in. (30 cm)

WHERE is it from?
Western Pacific: from Ryukyu Islands to Taiwan, with another population from New Caledonia to Queensland, Australia.

WHERE does it live in the wild?
Adults are found over sandy areas and among coral rubble, or close to caves and overhangs on shallow reefs. Juveniles are secretive and often found near reef walls.

WHAT aquarium environment?
Plenty of open water but with some large caves to provide shelter and sleeping places. Has no particular requirements with respect to lighting.

WHAT minimum size tank?
72 x 24 x 24 in. (180 x 60 x 60 cm)

WHAT does it eat?
Feeds readily on most frozen meaty foods (krill, shrimp, squid, mysis, for example) and will usually adapt to eat flake and pellets. Should be fed at least once daily.

HOW hardy?
Generally a robust species, but smaller individuals tend to adapt more easily to the aquarium than large ones, and those originating from the Australian population appear to be somewhat hardier than others.

▲ *The harlequin tuskfish is a relatively peaceful, larger wrasse that can be kept in a reef aquarium.*

HOW compatible with other fishes?
Juveniles are generally peaceful toward unrelated species, but become bolder and more aggressive as they mature. Smaller or more docile species may be bullied, and very small fish tankmates may even be eaten. Best kept with large, robust fishes. Do not keep it with others of its own species.

HOW compatible with invertebrates?
Harmless to sessile invertebrates and poses less of a threat than other large wrasses to snails, starfishes, and hermit crabs. However, it is likely to eat shrimps and small crabs.

WHAT does it cost?
★★★☆☆ ★★★★☆

Pseudocoris heteroptera

Torpedo wrasse

PROFILE

The torpedo wrasse is a relatively uncommon but very attractive species (particularly the males), and an excellent fish for the larger reef aquarium. This species has two distinct color phases: Females are silvery-white, with darker longitudinal stripes. The male, however, is spectacularly colorful, with a deep blue-green head, and a bright yellow-green body overlaid with dark blue bands. The color in both sexes can vary considerably according to mood.

WHAT size?
8 in. (20 cm)

WHERE is it from?
Wide range across Indian and Pacific oceans.

WHERE does it live in the wild?
This species lives in aggregations of one terminal phase male and several initial phase individuals on outer reef crests, generally feeding on zooplankton high in the water column.

► The torpedo wrasse (Pseudocoris heteroptera), *especially in its terminal phase as shown here, is a beautiful, active fish for a large reef tank.*

WHAT aquarium environment?
Needs plenty of open water but also some caves and crevices to provide shelter, particularly when first added to the aquarium. No specific requirements with respect to lighting.

WHAT minimum size tank?
48 x 24 x 24 in. (120 x 60 x 60 cm)

WHAT does it eat?
Feeds readily on frozen and dry foods. Prefers frozen crustaceans (krill, chopped shrimp, copepods, mysis, brineshrimp). Feed twice a day, or preferably more often.

HOW hardy?
Usually hardy, may jump from open aquariums.

HOW compatible with other fishes?
Generally peaceful with other fishes. Can usually be kept with other planktivorous wrasses, although males may occasionally harass such tankmates. Groups of one male and several females can be kept in large tanks. May be shy when first added to the aquarium and should not be kept with aggressive species.

HOW compatible with invertebrates?
Harmless to almost all invertebrates; large individuals may occasionally eat small shrimps.

WHAT does it cost?
★★☆☆☆

Thalassoma bifasciatum

Bluehead wrasse

The bluehead wrasse is one of the most common fishes of the tropical west Atlantic, and is notable for the profound color changes that it undergoes with age, sex, and social status. Within a group, most individuals are yellow with white bellies, sometimes with a longitudinal black band separating the yellow and white. These fishes may be male or female (and females can turn into males). This color pattern is known as the initial phase, and is also characteristic of juveniles. The color scheme also gives rise to this fish's alternative common name of banana wrasse. Mature males look completely different: Their coloration (known as the terminal phase) is a bright blue head and deep green rear half of the body, with two black bands, separated by a light blue band, in between.

WHAT size?
10 in. (25 cm).

WHERE is it from?
Western Atlantic: Caribbean Sea, Florida, and Gulf of Mexico, northern coast of South America.

WHERE does it live in the wild?
The bluehead wrasse lives in large groups, hovering above the reef feeding on zooplankton.

WHAT aquarium environment?
Plenty of open water but with some caves and crevices to provide shelter and sleeping places. No specific requirements with respect to lighting.

WHAT minimum size tank?
60 x 24 x 24 in. (150 x 60 x 60 cm)

WHAT does it eat?
Feeds readily on frozen and dry foods. Frozen crustaceans (krill, chopped shrimp, copepods, mysis, brineshrimp) provide a good match to its natural diet. Should be fed twice a day, or preferably more often.

▼ *A terminal phase male bluehead wrasse is a very attractive fish.*

HOW hardy?
Usually a very hardy, robust species.

HOW compatible with other fishes?
Requires fairly robust tankmates, as it may harass less assertive species, particularly if they are introduced when it is already established in the aquarium. Groups of one terminal phase male and several initial phase individuals can be kept in large tanks.

HOW compatible with invertebrates?
Harmless to almost all invertebrates; large individuals may eat small shrimps, particularly if not kept well fed.

WHAT does it cost?
★★★☆☆

Thalassoma lucasanum

Rainbow wrasse

PROFILE

The rainbow wrasse comes from a rather unusual area for an aquarium fish, namely the eastern Pacific. As a result, it is relatively uncommon in the aquarium trade. However, it is a very attractive species and well worth keeping in a suitable reef aquarium.

In common with the bluehead wrasse *(Thalassoma bifasciatum)* it has different color phases, but unlike that species, its common name applies equally well to both phases. Initial phase females and juveniles of both sexes are yellow with longitudinal red and blackish stripes. The terminal phase males (larger than initial phase fishes) have a blue-green head with some pinkish markings, a broad bright yellow band behind the head, a pinkish-red rear half of the body, and a blue-green tail.

WHAT size?
6 in. (15 cm)

WHERE is it from?
Eastern Pacific: Gulf of California to Panama and the Galapagos.

WHERE does it live in the wild?
This species is usually found over shallow reefs, but does range as deep as 130 ft. (40 m). It lives in large groups, with a few terminal phase males and many more initial

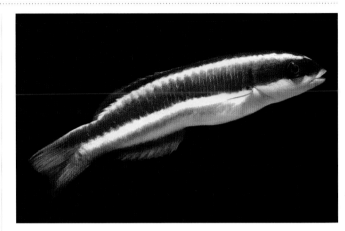

▲ *An initial phase rainbow wrasse. Terminal phase males look very different.*

phase fishes. It feeds mainly on zooplankton, but will also eat benthic invertebrates.

WHAT aquarium environment?
Prefers plenty of swimming space, but needs some caves and crevices to provide shelter and sleeping places. No specific requirements with respect to lighting.

WHAT minimum size tank?
48 x 18 x 18 in. (120 x 45 x 45 cm)

WHAT does it eat?
Will eat most frozen and dry foods; frozen crustaceans are a good substitute for the zooplankton it eats in the wild. Should be fed twice a day, or preferably more often.

HOW hardy?
A very hardy, robust species. Jumping from open-topped aquariums is the major threat to its health.

HOW compatible with other fishes?
Generally peaceful toward other species. Groups of one terminal phase male and several initial phase individuals can be kept in large tanks.

HOW compatible with invertebrates?
Harmless to almost all invertebrates, although large individuals may eat small shrimps.

WHAT does it cost?
★★★☆☆

Tangs and surgeonfishes

The tang family (Acanthuridae) is one of the most important families of aquarium fishes. The tangs and surgeonfishes (the terms are used interchangeably here) are generally medium-to-large, highly active, often very colorful fishes. They have the great advantage for the reef aquarium keeper that, as herbivores, they have very little interest in invertebrates and are enthusiastic grazers of algae. They can therefore be a great help in preventing and dealing with blooms of nuisance algae.

This is not to say that tangs are entirely trouble free or that they can be kept in any aquarium. For one thing, their size precludes keeping even the smallest species in small tanks, particularly as they tend to be very active swimmers.

Tangs are physiologically so well adapted to eating algae (and in some cases detritus) that they are highly dependent on having it in their diet.

Most tangs will eat any food that they are offered, but unless their food, like algae, is rich in vitamins, they may develop health problems, most notably head and lateral line erosion. Fortunately, many foods based on algae are available. These include dried or salted seaweeds (sold either through the aquarium trade or for human food) and flake foods and pellets based either on marine algae or on spirulina.

Price guide

★	$24–48
★★	$48–64
★★★	$64–96
★★★★	$96–192
★★★★★	$400–960

▲ The long snout of this yellow tang (Zebrasoma flavescens) *enables it to reach into crevices on the reef to graze filamentous algae.*

▲ *Different tang species can be kept together in large aquariums, such as the purple* (Zebrasoma xanthurum)*, sailfin* (Z. desjardinii)*, and powder blue* (Acanthurus leucosternon)*, seen here feeding on dried seaweed.*

As a family, tangs are very susceptible to white spot *(Cryptocaryon irritans)* infections. Individual species vary in their vulnerability to these infections, but all tangs should be regarded as being likely to contract white spot, and precautions should be taken to minimize the chances of such infections.

Many tangs are quite territorial, particularly toward their own species and other tangs that look similar. This holds true even among species that are usually found in groups in the wild. To keep more than one tang in an aquarium, use a large tank (this tends to reduce inter-species aggression), choose fishes that are dissimilar in appearance and preferably among the less aggressive species, and stock them in a defined order from least to most territorial. Then keep them well fed—hungry fishes tend to be more aggressive toward perceived competitors.

As with many larger fishes, relatively small individuals tend to adapt more easily to aquarium life than full-grown adults. However, very small tangs can also be difficult to get established in the aquarium: 3–4 in. (7–10 cm) individuals are usually the best ones to buy.

Finally, a caution for fishkeepers: These fishes owe their family name to the fact that on their caudal peduncles (at the base of their tails) they carry razor-sharp blades. In most species these are kept sheathed most of the time, but they may be used as weapons of both offense and defense and can inflict nasty wounds on other fishes—and on fishkeepers. In some species these blades are venomous. When catching tangs, be careful not to come into contact with these blades, and watch out for them getting tangled in nets. It pays to watch the fishes carefully for signs of aggressive behavior when working in the aquarium, but tangs will usually either ignore their keeper's hands, or will hover around non-aggressively looking for anything edible that might appear.

Zebrasoma species

Sailfin tangs

The largest of the zebrasoma tangs, the sailfin tangs *Zebrasoma desjardinii* and *Z. veliferum,* have very large dorsal and anal fins, even by the standards of this genus—this is particularly evident in young specimens. The juveniles of the two species look very similar, but the differences become more obvious as the fishes mature.

These fishes generally have a relaxed disposition in the aquarium and relate well to people, often becoming real pets, in contrast to some tangs that can be rather nervous and jittery.

In dealers' tanks these species can look quite drab, but the subdued colors can be caused by the presence of copper in the water. Sailfin tangs can also change color dramatically according to mood. This is particularly notable in *Z. desjardinii*, where the base color can vary from pale gray through chestnut brown to almost black. Darker bands on the head can appear or disappear, and other markings can vary in intensity. The color changes can happen in a matter of seconds. Both species are among the best fishes for dealing with algae problems. They eat virtually any macroalgae and filamentous algae, as well as bubble algae and sometimes even cyanobacterial films.

WHERE do they live in the wild?
Typically found in lagoons and reef areas from shallow water to depths of 100 ft. (30 m); juveniles often live among branching stony corals.

WHAT aquarium environment?
Plenty of open water with some suitably large caves to provide shelter and sleeping places, and areas of rock for grazing.

WHAT do they eat?
Need a diet based primarily on algae (herbivore flake and pellets, dried seaweed sheets, spirulina-enriched brineshrimp).

HOW hardy?
Among the hardiest of all tangs, with a relatively low susceptibility to parasitic infections.

HOW compatible with other fishes?
Generally peaceful toward unrelated species. May squabble

Red Sea sailfin tang
Zebrasoma desjardinii ▷

An excellent fish for a large tank. It is beautiful, interesting, hardy, and will make short work of hair algae and bubble algae problems.

WHAT size? *16 in. (40 cm)*
WHAT min size tank? *72 x 24 x 24 in. (180 x 60 x 60 cm)*
WHERE is it from? *Red Sea and Indian Ocean.*

with other tangs but fights are not usually serious. However, should not be kept with others of their own species, nor should the two species of sailfin tang be kept together.

HOW compatible with invertebrates?
Normally harmless to all invertebrates: when extremely hungry, may occasionally browse on small, low-growing polyps.

WHAT do they cost?
★☆☆☆☆ ★★☆☆☆
This price range refers to the two species featured on these pages.

Pacific sailfin tang
Zebrasoma veliferum

Very similar to Z. desjardinii *(some authorities consider them to be geographical variants of a single species), this species is usually less expensive and shares all the virtues of its Red Sea cousin.*

WHAT size? 16 in. (40 cm)
WHAT min size tank? 72 x 24 x 24 in. (180 x 60 x 60 cm)
WHERE is it from? *Wide range across the Pacific Ocean from Indonesia to Hawaii, as far north as southern Japan, south to New Caledonia.*

▼ *The adult* Z. desjardinii *is more colorful and arguably more attractive than* Z. veliferum.

▼ *Juveniles of the two sailfin tang species are very similar. The purple color around the tail spines suggests that this is a young* Z. desjardinii.

▲ *As an adult,* Z. veliferum *is easy to distinguish from its Red Sea and Indian Ocean cousin.*

ZEBRASOMA TANGS

A small genus with just eight species, *Zebrasoma* is disproportionately important in the marine aquarium trade: Six of the eight species are very common aquarium fishes. These tangs have a characteristic morphology, with long snouts, short bodies, and very tall dorsal and anal fins.

Zebrasoma flavescens

Yellow tang

PROFILE

One of the most popular marine aquarium fishes, this beautiful lemon-yellow species is one of the best tangs for most reef aquariums. It is an excellent algae grazer, generally peaceful toward unrelated species (it is one of the less aggressive *Zebrasoma* species) and is one of the few tangs that can be kept in groups (although a large tank is needed for this). It is the smallest of the *Zebrasoma* tangs.

WHAT size?
8 in. (20 cm)

WHERE is it from?
Pacific Ocean: Hawaii, Ryukyu Islands, Marianas, Marshall Islands, and Wake Islands.

WHERE does it live in the wild?
In lagoons and on seaward reefs, in coral-rich areas, browsing algae from rocks. Usually found singly or in small groups.

WHAT aquarium environment?
Plenty of rocks and invertebrates to provide cover and (in the case of rocks) grazing opportunities. Has less need for open water than many other tangs, and will adapt well to a densely stocked reef aquarium.

WHAT minimum size tank?
48 x 18 x 18 in. (120 x 45 x 45 cm)

WHAT does it eat?
Will browse algae from rocks in the aquarium, but this should be supplemented with a diet based on dried seaweed and algae-based dry foods.

HOW hardy?
Generally robust given a good diet, but should be watched carefully for white spot infections.

HOW compatible with other fishes?
Generally peaceful toward unrelated species, and will usually tolerate other tangs provided that the aquarium is reasonably large. It should not be kept with other yellow-colored tangs (juveniles of *Acanthurus olivaceus, A. coeruleus,* and *A. pyroferus,* for example) or with its own kind—except in groups. Keeping five or more yellow tangs together is possible in large tanks (at least 60 x 24 x 24 in. [150 x 60 x 60 cm]), when all individuals are introduced together.

HOW compatible with invertebrates?
Usually completely safe with all invertebrates.

WHAT does it cost?
★☆☆☆☆

▼ *The yellow tang is an excellent reef aquarium fish, easy to keep and justifiably very popular.*

Zebrasoma xanthurum

Purple tang

PROFILE

This is a stunningly beautiful species: Although its color scheme is simple, the purple color on the body has an amazing depth in healthy individuals and the yellow of the tail, pectoral fins, nostrils, and lips is a perfect counterpoint. Its full beauty is not always apparent in dealers' tanks, as the color can fade somewhat if there is copper in the water. Because of its origins in the Middle East, this is an expensive species. Its temperament means that it should be stocked with care; usually it should be the last fish added to the aquarium, after less aggressive species. It is a highly effective grazer for controlling hair algae blooms.

WHAT size?
9 in. (22 cm)

WHERE is it from?
Red Sea and Persian Gulf; also reported in the Maldives.

WHERE does it live in the wild?
In coral-rich areas and over rocky seabeds and slopes, grazing filamentous algae.

WHAT aquarium environment?
A balance of plenty of swimming space and some rocks and invertebrates to provide shelter.

WHAT minimum size tank?
72 x 24 x 24 in. (180 x 60 x 60 cm)

WHAT does it eat?
Dried algae sheets should be the staple diet, supplemented by other algae-based foods and grazing algae within the aquarium.

HOW hardy?
Generally hardy and adapts well to life in the aquarium. Less susceptible than most other tangs to white spot. Large adults do not settle in as easily as smaller individuals.

HOW compatible with other fishes?
When established in the aquarium, it can become highly territorial toward other tangs

▲ *The purple tang is a beautiful fish and an excellent grazer for the reef tank, helping to keep the live rock free of hair algae.*

(especially other *Zebrasoma* species) and other fishes of similar appearance. Occasionally becomes aggressive toward completely unrelated fishes, and often becomes the dominant individual in the aquarium. Keeping it in a large aquarium can minimize conflicts.

HOW compatible with invertebrates?
Almost always safe with all invertebrates.

WHAT does it cost?
★★★★☆

Zebrasoma rostratum

Black tang

The black tang is one of the few all-black marine fishes—in a healthy juvenile the black is particularly deep and solid, the only non-black part of the fish being the blades on the caudal peduncle, which are bright white. As the fish matures it develops a silvery-green sheen on the back, but remains a highly attractive species.

The black tang is an extremely expensive species (among *Zebrasoma* tangs only the almost-unobtainable *Z. gemmatum* commands a higher price), which is seen by those who like fishes for their rarity as an advantage, and by those who like them for their beauty rather differently! The reasons for the high price are not that the fish is uncommon, but because its natural range is outside areas that are regularly worked by collectors of fishes for the aquarium trade. Fortunately, it is a robust, hardy species, so the high price paid for it is unlikely to be money wasted, provided that it is cared for properly.

WHAT size?
8.5 in. (21 cm)

WHERE is it from?
Eastern central Pacific Ocean: Line Islands, Marquesas, Society Islands, Tuamoto, and Pitcairn.

WHERE does it live in the wild?
In lagoons and on reef slopes.

WHAT aquarium environment?
Balance of open water for swimming space and rocks and invertebrates for cover.

WHAT minimum size tank?
48 x 24 x 24 in. (120 x 60 x 60 cm)

WHAT does it eat?
The diet should be based on algae: dried algae sheets and algae-based dry foods. Will also graze filamentous algae growing in the aquarium.

HOW hardy?
The relatively limited experience with this species suggests that it is generally quite a hardy species,

▲ *The black tang is an excellent reef aquarium fish, marred only by its high price.*

once it has become established in the aquarium and recovered from a very long journey from its native range.

HOW compatible with other fishes?
One of the least territorial *Zebrasoma* tangs, unlikely to bother unrelated species. May be picked on by more aggressive tangs.

HOW compatible with invertebrates?
Usually harmless to invertebrates.

WHAT does it cost?
★★★★★

Zebrasoma scopas

Scopas tang

PROFILE

The scopas tang is less brightly colored than most other *Zebrasoma* species, but remains a popular aquarium species. Its color scheme is very variable between individuals, and even in the same fish can change over time. Although most scopas tangs have a relatively muted coloration in black and brown, they can be all black (such variants are sometimes sold as *Z. rostratum*, the true black tang, which commands a price up to 20 times higher than the scopas tang) or have varying amounts of yellow on the body. These colors usually change to the more standard scheme over time.

The scopas tang has the same high-finned, long-nosed profile as other *Zebrasoma* species. It is an excellent species for controlling filamentous algae blooms, and will also eat macroalgae, some of which can also cause problems in the reef aquarium.

WHAT size?
8 in. (20 cm)

WHERE is it from?
Indian and Pacific Oceans: from East Africa to Tuamoto, as far north as Japan, south to Lord Howe Island.

▶ *The scopas tang is more subtly colored than other* Zebrasoma *species.*

WHERE does it live in the wild?
Lagoons and reef slopes, from very shallow water to depths of 66 ft. (20 m) or so. Juveniles live singly, always close to cover, adults range widely over the reef and can be found singly or in pairs, or occasionally in large groups, sometimes mixed with other tangs.

WHAT aquarium environment?
Needs plenty of swimming space (hence larger tanks than their size would suggest) plus some rocks and invertebrates for cover.

WHAT minimum size tank?
60 x 24 x 24 in. (150 x 60 x 60 cm)

WHAT does it eat?
The usual tang vegetarian diet: dried algae as sheets or flakes, algae-based flake or pellet foods.

HOW hardy?
Generally robust, but has the usual tang susceptibility to white spot infections—more so than some other *Zebrasoma* species.

HOW compatible with other fishes?
One of the most aggressive *Zebrasoma* species, highly territorial toward other tangs. Unrelated species, if not perceived as competitors, are usually ignored. Keeping it in a large aquarium also helps to reduce its aggressiveness.

HOW compatible with invertebrates?
Almost always safe with all invertebrates.

WHAT does it cost?
★☆☆☆☆

Ctenochaetus strigosus and *C. truncatus*

Kole and silver-spot tangs

The kole and silver-spot tangs are very similar in appearance apart from the fact that the Kole tang *(Ctenochaetus strigosus)* has fine pinstripes over its chocolate-brown base color and the silver spot tang *(C. truncatus)* has a dense scatter of tiny light dots. It has been suggested that they are geographical variants of the same species. Neither species tends to look its best in dealers' tanks, as the base color of the body can become very washed out in water containing copper. Even quite pale individuals can rapidly regain their color once in a normal reef aquarium environment.

WHERE do they live in the wild?
Over areas of coral, rock, and rubble, usually solitary, but sometimes in small groups, feeding mainly on detritus.

WHAT aquarium environment?
Prefer plenty of live rock to provide grazing opportunities.

WHAT do they eat?
Will eat seaweed sheets and dry foods, but also graze microalgae films from rocks and aquarium glass and eat detritus.

HOW hardy?
Quite susceptible to white spot infections; should preferably be quarantined before being added to the display aquarium. Otherwise hardy.

HOW compatible with other fishes?
Usually peaceful with other fishes, including other tangs. Should not be kept with others of their own species.

HOW compatible with invertebrates?
Almost always safe with all invertebrates.

WHAT do they cost?
★☆☆☆☆   ★★☆☆☆

Silver-spot tang
Ctenochaetus truncatus

This species has become widely available only relatively recently. It shares all the virtues of the kole tang, although it is still not as common in the aquarium trade, and so is less familiar to fishkeepers.

WHAT size? 6.5 in. (16 cm)
WHAT min size tank? 48 x 18 x 15 in. (120 x 45 x 38 cm)
WHERE is it from?
Indian Ocean.

CTENOCHAETUS TANGS

The *Ctenochaetus* tangs differ from the other tangs in that the main part of their diet in the wild is detritus, supplemented by microalgae. Rather than snipping off fronds of filamentous algae or macroalgae using clipperlike mouthparts, they scrape microalgae and detritus from hard surfaces using brushlike teeth that line their large lips—this is a feeding method more associated with herbivorous blennies than other tangs. They include among their number the smallest of the tangs, and the fact that they need less swimming space than most of their relatives makes them more suitable for medium-sized tanks than other species that are more active.

Closely related to the kole tang, C. truncatus *has spots instead of stripes.*

Kole, or yellow-eye, tang
Ctenochaetus strigosus

A long-time favorite of marine fishkeepers, this a peaceful, attractive, inexpensive species that spends its time grazing detritus and microalgae—often leaving characteristic "kiss" marks on the aquarium glass.

WHAT size? 6 in. (15 cm)
WHAT min size tank? 48 x 18 x 15 in. (120 x 45 x 38 cm)
WHERE is it from? Eastern central Pacific Ocean: Hawaii and Johnston Atoll; also around Australia in western Pacific Ocean.

Ctenochaetus hawaiiensis

Chevron tang

PROFILE

This species undergoes a dramatic color change with age: Juveniles are bright orange with vivid purple stripes arranged in a chevron pattern, whereas adults are black with fine stripes. Like *Zebrasoma* tangs, this species has impressively large fins, and even the less colorful adults are spectacular fishes. Chevron tangs are usually sold as juveniles; they are quite expensive, as they are collected in deep water. Like other *Ctenochaetus* tangs, they spend most of their time grazing, picking up detritus from sand and rock surfaces and grazing microalgal films, including from the aquarium glass.

WHAT size?
10 in. (25 cm)

WHERE is it from?
Pacific Ocean, from Micronesia to Hawaii and Pitcairn Islands.

WHERE does it live in the wild?
In lagoons and on reef slopes.

WHAT aquarium environment?
Appreciates plenty of rocks and caves for grazing and shelter; mature tanks with some detritus are best.

WHAT minimum size tank?
60 x 24 x 24 in. (150 x 60 x 60 cm)

WHAT does it eat?
Will graze microalgae films and eat detritus in the aquarium; will also eat dried seaweed sheets and other dry foods.

HOW hardy?
Vulnerable to white spot and velvet disease—will not usually be the first fish affected in an outbreak, but once infected tends to deteriorate rapidly.

HOW compatible with other fishes?
Usually peaceful with unrelated species and usually tolerates other tangs. Should not be kept with others of its own kind.

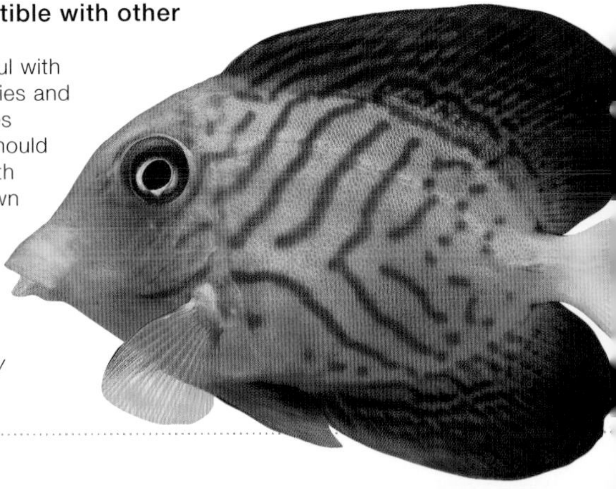

▶ *Juvenile chevron tangs are spectacularly colored.*

▲ *This subadult chevron tang could easily be taken to be a completely different species from the juvenile form shown below.*

HOW compatible with invertebrates?
Generally completely safe with invertebrates; may occasionally pick at mucus on corals or *Tridacna* clams.

WHAT does it cost?
★★★★☆

Ctenochaetus tominiensis

Orangetipped bristletooth

PROFILE

This species is very distinctive, with its white tail and bright golden dorsal and anal fins. It is probably the smallest of the entire tang family, and is usually a very peaceful, relaxed species, spending its time working its way over the substrate picking at detritus and algal films. It is a relative newcomer to the aquarium trade, and may be quite hard to find for sale, but it is usually inexpensive.

WHAT size?
6.5 in. (16 cm)

WHERE is it from?
Western central Pacific Ocean: from Indonesia and the Philippines to northern Great Barrier Reef, Solomon Islands, Palau, Vanuatu, Fiji, and Tonga.

WHERE does it live in the wild?
Found on steep, coral-rich drop-offs, in small groups.

WHAT aquarium environment?
Plenty of live rock to provide grazing opportunities.

WHAT minimum size tank?
48 x 18 x 15 in. (120 x 45 x 38 cm)

WHAT does it eat?
Algae-based diet: dried seaweed sheets or flakes, algae-based dry foods. Also grazes algae and detritus on live rock and sand beds.

HOW hardy?
Reasonably hardy: is susceptible to white spot infections, but not excessively so.

HOW compatible with other fishes?
Peaceful with other fishes; may be bullied by more aggressive tangs.

HOW compatible with invertebrates?
Usually ignores all invertebrates.

WHAT does it cost?
★☆☆☆☆

This species is also known as the tomini tang. It is a good choice for a medium-sized reef aquarium.

Acanthurus pyroferus and *A. tristis*

Mimic tangs

PROFILE

The two species of mimic tang *(Acanthurus pyroferus and A. tristis)* are notable because their juveniles mimic *Centropyge* angelfishes. The mimicry is very precise; the juvenile tangs copy the body shapes, color schemes, and even fin shapes of the angels. It is believed that the mimicry serves to deter predators from eating the juvenile tangs; these species have relatively small caudal blades and dwarf angels are better armed, with long spines on the gill covers.

As the tangs grow, they presumably no longer need the protection offered by the mimicry, which is probably less convincing when the tangs have outgrown the angels. As well as changing color when maturing, their bodies elongate somewhat and their tail fins change shape completely from convex to lyre-shaped.

ACANTHURUS TANGS

Acanthurus is the largest genus of tangs (with 38 species) and includes some very diverse species in terms of color, size, geographical origins—and aquarium care. Among the *Acanthurus* species that are kept in the aquarium are the most aggressive and most peaceful tangs, the easiest and most difficult to keep, and many beautiful species.

WHERE do they live in the wild?
In shallow lagoons and on reefs, typically around the base in areas of mixed rock, sand, and coral.

WHAT aquarium environment?
Plenty of rocks and invertebrates, but some swimming space: do not need so much open water as most other tangs.

WHAT do they eat?
Dried algae sheets should form their staple diet; algae-based flake and pellet foods are also useful. Will eat almost all foods that are offered.

HOW hardy?
Among the most hardy of their family, provided that they receive a good algae-based diet. For *Acanthurus* species, they have a relatively low susceptibility to white spot *(Cryptocaryon)* infections.

HOW compatible with other fishes?
Very peaceful by tang standards; however, they should not be kept with their own species. May be bullied by more aggressive tangs, particularly other *Acanthurus* species.

HOW compatible with invertebrates?
Almost always safe with all invertebrates.

WHAT do they cost?
★☆☆☆☆ ★★☆☆☆

Indian Ocean mimic tang
Acanthurus tristis

This species mimics Eibl's angelfish (Centropyge eibli) as a juvenile, but as it matures it undergoes a dramatic transformation to become brown with a light face, a dark ring around the eye, a black mark on the gill cover, and dark dorsal, anal, and caudal fins.

WHAT size? *10 in. (25 cm)*
WHAT min size tank? *48 x 24 x 24 in. (120 x 60 x 60 cm)*
WHERE is it from? *Indian Ocean: Bay of Bengal, Andaman Sea, Maldives, Chagos Islands, and southern Indonesia.* ▽

▼▲ *This subadult* Acanthurus tristis *(shown below) still shows traces of the juvenile pattern that enables it to mimic the angelfish* Centropyge eibli *(shown above).*

△

Mimic tang
Acanthurus pyroferus

As a juvenile, Acanthurus pyroferus *mimics two dwarf angelfish species, the black-and-white, half-black, or pearlscale, angel (Centropyge vroliki) and the lemonpeel angel (C. flavissima). In adult coloration it is yellowish brown to chocolate brown—an alternative common name is chocolate surgeonfish.*

WHAT size? *10 in. (25 cm)*
WHAT min size tank? *48 x 24 x 24 in. (120 x 60 x 60 cm)*
WHERE is it from? *Indian and Pacific Oceans, from the Seychelles east to the Marquesas and Tuamoto, north to southern Japan and south to Great Barrier Reef and New Caledonia.*

▲ *This form of the mimic tang has a color scheme very similar to that of the half-black angel, Centropyge vroliki. The mimicry is so convincing that this fish was on sale as an angel.*

▼ *Adult mimic tangs are more soberly colored than juveniles.*

Acanthurus leucosternon

Powder blue tang

PROFILE

This is an absolutely stunning species, a longtime favorite of marine fishkeepers, a coral reef icon—and a difficult fish to keep long term, because it takes the few undesirable attributes of the tang family to extremes. It is highly territorial and will attack most other tangs and even unrelated species if they are perceived as competitors. This may be related to behavior in the wild: Individuals or pairs will sometimes tend "gardens" of filamentous algae, which they defend fiercely against raids by other herbivorous fishes, tangs included. However, territoriality is not the only issue with this species. Even by tang standards, it is highly susceptible to white spot. Despite these difficulties, its sheer beauty makes it a highly desirable species, and with care it can be kept successfully.

WHAT size?
10 in. (25 cm).

WHERE is it from?
Indian Ocean: East Africa to the Andaman Sea; also to Bali in the western Pacific.

WHERE does it live in the wild?
Found in shallow water over reef flats and upper reef slopes, usually singly or in mated pairs. Occasionally form large aggregations to feed en masse.

WHAT aquarium environment?
Plenty of open swimming space, but some rocks for shelter; strong currents and high water quality are best.

WHAT minimum size tank?
60 x 24 x 24 in. (150 x 60 x 60 cm)

WHAT does it eat?
The diet should be based primarily on algae: Dried seaweed sheets should be the staple, supplemented with spirulina or kelp-based dry foods.

HOW hardy?
A major issue with this species is susceptibility to white spot *(Cryptocaryon irritans)* infections; these happen most frequently soon after introduction to a new aquarium, but can occur at other times of stress. Quarantining the fish before introduction to the aquarium can help, but when keeping this species it is essential to have facilities in place ready to treat infections when they occur.

HOW compatible with other fishes?
Highly territorial and aggressive toward both related species, fishes of similar color, and others perceived as competing for food.

HOW compatible with invertebrates?
Almost always safe with all corals and clams; very occasionally will eat small, low-growing polyps like star polyps *(Pachyclavularia* species).

WHAT does it cost?
★★☆☆☆

◄ *The popularity of this stunning species belies the fact that it is quite difficult to keep.*

Acanthurus
Conv

Acanthurus japonicus
Powder brown tang

The convict t
colored than
the family, bu
beauty. In a h
individual, the
silvery-bronze
stripes are a v
Among *Acant*
is one of the
for the aquari
and more pea
most, and a g
controlling nu
It has an extr
geographic di
very abundan
an important
areas. Despite
suitability as
it is an uncon
dealers' shop
inexpensive w

WHAT size
11 in. (27 cr

WHERE is
Throughout
(except arou
peninsula) a
from East A
California.

WHERE d
wild?
In lagoons a
hard substra
near freshwa
(where algae
juveniles ofte
pools. May f
to graze alga

PROFILE

This is one of the more peaceful of the *Acanthurus* tangs, despite being similar in body shape, ecology, and behavior to highly aggressive species such as the powder blue and Achilles tangs (*A. leucosternon* and *A. achilles*, respectively). Its coloration is not so gaudy as that of those other species (and it is not so expensive), but it remains a highly attractive fish.

A similar species is sometimes sold under the same common names as *A. japonicus*—this is *A. nigricans*, which is another attractive species but is regarded as more delicate and harder to keep than *A. japonicus*. The two species can be distinguished by the fact that *A. nigricans* tends to have darker and more even coloration on the flanks, and the white mark on the face is a simple bar under the eye rather than covering most of the side of the face, as in *A. japonicus*.

WHAT size?
8.5 in. (21 cm)

WHERE is it from?
West Pacific, from Sulawesi in Indonesia to Ryukyu Islands in southern Japan and the Philippines.

▲ *This species is more straightforward to keep than the powder blue tang and more subtly attractive.*

WHERE does it live in the wild?
In shallow exposed areas in lagoons and on reefs. Often found in small groups.

WHAT aquarium environment?
Rocks and invertebrates for cover and plenty of swimming space. Prefers strong currents and well-oxygenated water.

WHAT minimum size tank?
48 x 24 x 24 in. (120 x 60 x 60 cm)

WHAT does it eat?
Should be fed an algae-based diet: dried seaweed sheets and flakes, other algae-based dry foods. May require a supply of filamentous algae in the tank to stimulate feeding when new to the aquarium.

HOW hardy?
Generally reasonably hardy but still requires careful husbandry; moderately susceptible to white spot infection but not one of the most vulnerable of the family.

HOW compatible with other fishes?
One of the less aggressive *Acanthurus* species, this species is not particularly territorial and is unlikely to cause any major problems with other species. However, more aggressive tangs may pick on it.

HOW compatible with invertebrates?
Very unlikely to harm any invertebrates.

WHAT does it cost?
★★☆☆☆ ★★★☆☆

Blue

GOBIES

GOBIES

F

The blue ta
Caribbean
family that
the aquariu
of this spec
that varies
the fish's m
bright yello
around the
matures, it
rather dull
until the bl
young adul
with yellow
this specie
for sea turl
from their :
the aquaril
species for
blooms.

Gobies

▶ The gobies (Gobiidae) are one of the largest families of fishes, with over 2,000 known species. A characteristic of the family is that the pelvic fins are fused together to form a sucker, which allows gobies to cling on to rocks and other hard substrates. Most gobies do not have swimbladders, so sink when they are not actively swimming, and the lateral line sensory system is usually absent, replaced by sensory ducts on the head.

Most gobies are relatively small (the largest known grow to around 12 in. [30 cm]) and the family includes some of the smallest of all known fishes; these attain an adult size of around $1/2$ in. (1 cm). Gobies are predominantly fishes of marine habitats and some are very attractive. Many make excellent reef aquarium fishes. Not all of them are easy to keep (although many are), but it is possible to find gobies to suit most reef tanks.

Price guide

★	$16–24
★★	$24–32
★★★	$32–40
★★★★	$40–48
★★★★★	$48–72

PROFILE

A wide range of gobies live in symbiotic relationships with pistol shrimps. The shrimps dig extensive burrows in sand, silt, and gravel seabeds, and the gobies occupy the burrows with the shrimps. The shrimps construct and maintain the burrows, and the gobies hover or sit close to the entrance, keeping watch for predators. In some cases, the gobies remain in contact with the shrimps' long antennae, and signal to them with flicks of the tail fin. Although not all gobies that associate with pistol shrimps do well in the aquarium, there are many that make great reef tank inhabitants.

The best way to keep shrimp gobies in the aquarium is with their partner shrimps, and it is sometimes possible to buy the shrimps and gobies together. More commonly, however, the gobies are sold without the shrimps (it is much harder to capture the latter). Although the gobies will live perfectly well without their shrimps, it is a pity not to be able to observe the relationship.

It is possible, but not easy, to buy the shrimp and the goby separately and get them to associate. To do this, the shrimp and goby should be placed together, at the same time, in a small aquarium, and allowed to remain there until they bond—a small

Amblyeleotris species

Shrimp gobies

tank is needed in order to get the shrimp and goby to come into contact. After a period in the small tank, they can be transferred to the main display aquarium, preferably using the same bag or container to move both partners. It is worth noting that not all shrimps will bond with all gobies; sometimes when added to the aquarium, a goby may find a shrimp's burrow but the shrimp will not tolerate the goby. All in all, it is much better to buy gobies and shrimps together when they are available.

▲ *Shrimp gobies live in close relationships with pistol shrimps. Here a clown goby* (Stonogobiops yasha) *shares a burrow with a golden pistol shrimp* (Alpheus ochrostriatus) *in a nano-reef aquarium.*

Amblyeleotris species
Amblyeleotris shrimp gobies

PROFILE

The *Amblyeleotris* shrimp gobies are peaceable and quite passive species that usually do well in the aquarium, with or without shrimp partners. They are generally rather quiet species, often spending much of the day resting, but paradoxically they are also great escapologists, jumping out of the tank through small gaps in the covers, and going over weirs into overflow chambers and sumps. If they are not kept with shrimps, they tend to adopt caves in live rock as a home, rather than dig their own burrows.

WHERE do they live in the wild?
In lagoons and on seaward reefs, on sand patches, from shallow water to depths of around 130 ft. (40 m).

WHAT aquarium environment?
Some live rock, and a mixed sand and gravel bed for constructing burrows (with the aid of shrimp partners); caves and crevices, particularly if kept without shrimps.

WHAT do they eat?
Will eat most dry and frozen foods, but present the food close to the bottom of the tank. Feed at least twice daily.

HOW hardy?
Generally very hardy; the main threat to them is jumping out of the aquarium.

HOW compatible with other fishes?
Very peaceful; will usually tolerate other shrimp gobies and even their own species, although they may quarrel but without any serious aggression. Prefer quiet tankmates: may hide if kept in tanks with many large or boisterous fishes.

HOW compatible with invertebrates?
Harmless to invertebrates.

WHAT do they cost?
★★★☆☆

Red-striped shrimp goby
Amblyeleotris fasciata

One of the smaller Amblyeleotris *species, this is very much typical of the genus as a whole: peaceful, quite passive, and well behaved in the reef aquarium.*

WHAT size? *3 in. (8 cm)*
WHAT min size tank? *36 x 15 x 15 in. (90 x 38 x 38 cm)*
WHERE is it from? *Christmas Island in the eastern Indian Ocean to Samoa in the western Pacific Ocean, north to the Ryukyu Islands, south to the Great Barrier Reef.*

Sun-tailed goby
Amblyeleotris yanoi

Although this species is very much a typical Amblyeleotris *species, long and slender with orange-red bands on a white body, its multicolored tail fin makes it instantly identifiable.*

WHAT size? *5 in. (13 cm)*
WHAT min size tank? *48 x 18 x 15 in. (120 x 45 x 38 cm)*
WHERE is it from? *Western Pacific Ocean: Ryukyu Islands, Bali, and Flores in Indonesia.*

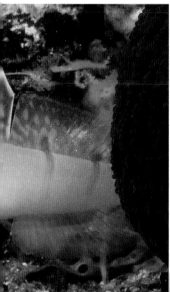

Tangerine goby
Amblyeleotris randalli

This is an unmistakable species, with its narrow orange bands and large, flaglike dorsal fin decorated with a prominent eyespot. It is especially impressive when full grown (it is one of the larger Amblyeleotris species), although it is not usually imported at such a large size.

WHAT size? *5 in. (12 cm)*
WHAT min size tank? *48 x 18 x 15 in. (120 x 45 x 38 cm)*
WHERE is it from? *Western Pacific Ocean, from the Moluccas to the Solomon Islands, north to the Ryukyu Islands, south to the Great Barrier Reef.*

Orange-spotted shrimp goby
Amblyeleotris guttata

With a dark belly and its flanks covered in bright orange spots, this is another very distinctive shrimp goby.

WHAT size? *4.5 in. (11 cm)*
WHAT min size tank? *36 x 18 x 18 in. (90 x 45 x 45 cm)*
WHERE is it from? *Western Pacific Ocean: the Philippines to Samoa, north to the Ryukyu Islands, south to Australia.*

Cryptocentrus species
Watchman gobies

Although the term "watchman goby" could be applied to any of the shrimp gobies, it is usually used to describe the *Cryptocentrus* species. These are robust fishes, with big mouths, that pose more of a threat to small shrimps and fishes than other shrimp gobies do. However, they are typically more extroverted and better suited to life with larger and bolder tankmates. They are attractive fishes with large fins and appealing froglike faces, and some are brightly colored. They typically do well either with or without their shrimp companions.

WHERE do they live in the wild?

In sandy areas of lagoons and protected bays, sometimes among mangroves. Live singly or in pairs in burrows with pistol shrimps; the gobies typically hover just outside the burrow entrance.

WHAT aquarium environment?

Need areas of sand and coral gravel to build burrows (with or without the help of pistol shrimps) and some live rock—these gobies often like to dig underneath the edges of rocks.

WHAT do they eat?

Will eat dry and frozen foods— particularly larger frozen crustaceans, such as krill and mysis shrimps. Food should be presented close to the substrate. Feed at least twice daily.

HOW hardy?

Generally hardy; the main threat to them is jumping from open aquariums, or through gaps in aquarium covers.

HOW compatible with other fishes?

May bully other shrimp gobies and eat very small tankmates such as neon gobies. Can hold their own with most other species, although they may be shy when first introduced to a tank with boisterous companions.

HOW compatible with invertebrates?

Harmless to corals and clams, but may eat very small shrimps.

WHAT do they cost?

★★★☆☆   ★★★★☆

Pink-spotted watchman goby
Cryptocentrus leptocephalus

One of the largest, boldest, and most assertive shrimp gobies, this species is best kept with robust companions. It makes a striking addition to a suitable reef aquarium community, but should not be kept with small shrimps or very small fishes, which it will eat.

WHAT size? *5 in. (12 cm)*
WHAT min size tank? *48 x 18 x 15 in. (120 x 45 x 38 cm)*
WHERE is it from? *Western Pacific: Indonesia to New Caledonia, southern Japan to the Great Barrier Reef.*

▲ Cryptocentrus *gobies have big mouths and can eat small shrimps.*

▶ *Yellow watchman gobies can be kept in pairs, but must be bought as such for this to be successful.*

Yellow watchman goby
Cryptocentrus cinctus

Perhaps the most attractive of all shrimp gobies, this species is justifiably popular with its bright yellow coloration speckled with neon blue spots. Darker markings can appear under some circumstances, according to the fish's mood. This species is now being imported more frequently with its shrimp partners. Larger individuals seem to adapt better to the aquarium than small juveniles, which tend to be very shy.

WHAT size? *4 in. (10 cm)*
WHAT min size tank? *36 x 18 x 18 in. (90 x 45 x 45 cm)*
WHERE is it from? *Western Pacific: southern Japan to Singapore, Micronesia, and the Great Barrier Reef.*

Stonogobiops species

PROFILE

Whereas many aquarium fishes have been known to biologists for a couple of hundred years, *Stonogobiops* was described as a genus only in 1977 and there are currently only six known species, not all of which are imported: The two species described here are the most likely to be offered for sale. These are among the smallest of the shrimp gobies and make very good aquarium fishes, with or without their shrimp partners, provided their tankmates are appropriate. They have a tendency to jump over weirs and may take up residence in sumps and overflow chambers. They are sometimes sold with pistol shrimps, or in mated pairs, or even better as mated pairs together with a shrimp, which is the ideal way to buy them.

WHERE do they live in the wild?
Found in areas of coral rubble and sand patches at depths ranging from around 23–165 ft. (7–50 m), living in pairs, often in burrows with *Alpheus* species pistol shrimps (usually *A. randalli*); the gobies usually hover close to the burrow entrance.

WHAT aquarium environment?
Require a bed of mixed sand and coral gravel for constructing burrows.

WHAT do they eat?
Will eat all dry and frozen foods provided they are of sufficiently small size. Feed at least twice daily.

Barber pole goby
Stonogobiops nematodes

This is the most commonly available Stonogobiops *species. Its color scheme of a yellow face and white body with reddish-brown bands is found in two other species* S. dracula *and* S. xanthorhinica, *although these two species lack the long first dorsal ray found in* S. nematodes.

WHAT size? *2.5 in. (6 cm)*
WHAT min size tank? *24 x 12 x 12 in. (60 x 30 x 30 cm)*
WHERE is it from? *The Seychelles in the Indian Ocean, the Philippines and Bali in the western Pacific.*

HOW hardy?
Generally hardy and not especially prone to disease, but may jump from open aquariums, or through gaps in aquarium covers.

HOW compatible with other fishes?
Should not be kept with predatory fishes and may hide constantly if kept with boisterous or aggressive tankmates. Should be kept only with their own species if bought as mated pairs.

HOW compatible with invertebrates?
Harmless to all invertebrates. May be eaten by sea anemones and some large serpent stars.

WHAT do they cost?
★★★☆☆   ★★★★★

Clown goby
Stonogobiops yasha

This is a beautiful species, white with bright red markings and a tall first dorsal fin ray. It is one of the most attractive fishes available for the nano-reef aquarium. A relatively recent arrival in the aquarium trade, and still not common, it was formally identified as a species only in 2001.

WHAT size? *2 in. (5 cm)*
WHAT min size tank? *24 x 12 x 12 in. (60 x 30 x 30 cm)*
WHERE is it from? *Western Pacific: Ryukyu Islands.*

▲ *Striking coloration and an extraordinary dorsal fin make Stonogobiops yasha one of the most desirable shrimp gobies.*

▶ *This species has a surprisingly large mouth and, despite its small size, can eat brineshrimp and small mysis shrimp.*

Elacatinus species

Neon gobies and their relatives

PROFILE

The neon gobies and their relatives of the genus *Elacatinus* (formerly *Gobiosoma*) include some old aquarium favorites, as well as some less familiar species. There are 31 species, but only a few are regularly offered for sale in aquarium stores. These are very small, slender fishes, ideal for smaller reef aquariums. Some species grow to less than 3/4 in. (2 cm). In the wild, some *Elacatinus* gobies provide cleaning services to larger fishes, picking off parasites, loose scales, and skin, in much the same way that the better-known cleaner wrasses (*Labroides* species) do. Intriguingly, the color schemes of some of the cleaner gobies are quite similar to those of cleaner wrasses. Although larger fishes (except for very peaceful ones) tend not to make great companions for neon gobies, this cleaning behavior can be observed in the aquarium. Many of these gobies have been bred in the aquarium, and in some species those offered for sale are usually tank raised.

WHERE do they live in the wild?
Range from rocky shores and tide pools to depths of 150 ft. (45 m), although usually found in shallow water, living among coral heads, within sponges or even between the spines of large sea urchins. Often found singly or in large groups.

WHAT aquarium environment?
Prefer some caves or crevices for shelter, plenty of live rock, and sand beds to provide small prey (a refugium may also be useful in this respect).

WHAT do they eat?
Will eat any frozen or dry foods, provided they are sufficiently small. Feed at least twice daily.

HOW hardy?
Most species are reasonably hardy, although if stressed they can be quite susceptible to white spot (*Cryptocaryon* infection), perhaps surprisingly in those species that act as cleaners.

HOW compatible with other fishes?
May be eaten by larger predators (not all of which will recognize those species that are cleaners as being such) and boisterous, fast-moving companions may prevent them getting their share of food. Can be kept in groups (including groups of mixed *Elacatinus* species) in larger aquariums, but will fight with each other in smaller ones.

HOW compatible with invertebrates?
Harmless to invertebrates, but may be eaten by crabs, very large shrimps, some serpent stars, and even large-polyp stony corals and large mushroom anemones.

WHAT do they cost?
★☆☆☆☆

Neon goby
Elacatinus oceanops

One of the first marine fishes to be bred in the aquarium on a commercial scale, the neon goby is a lovely little fish that is ideal for a nano-reef aquarium. It will provide cleaning services to other fishes in the aquarium, and in a large aquarium can be kept in large groups (among which pairs will often form).

WHAT size? 2 in. (5 cm)
WHAT min size tank? 24 x 12 x 12 in. (60 x 30 x 30 cm)
WHERE is it from? Western Atlantic: from southern Florida to Texas, south to Belize.

▽

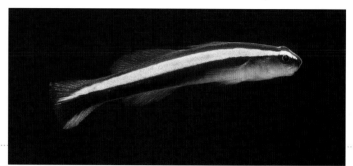

Green-banded goby
Elacatinus multifasciatus

*In the wild, this attractive little species is often found among the spines of large sea urchins, a situation that can be reproduced in the aquarium for those willing to keep a long-spined urchin (*Diadema *species).*

WHAT size? *2 in. (5 cm)*
WHAT min size tank? *24 x 12 x 12 in. (60 x 30 x 30 cm)*
WHERE is it from? *Western Atlantic: from the Bahamas to northern South America.*

Gold neon goby
Elacatinus randalli

This lovely species is another cleaner goby. It is often offered for sale at smaller sizes than the neon goby, and there are several similar species (not all of which enter the aquarium trade) with bright gold longitudinal stripes, including E. figaro, E. evelynae (in which the gold stripe does not extend the full length of the body), E. xanthipora, E. horsti, and E. phthirophagus, as well as hybrids between E. randalli *and* E. oceanops.

WHAT size? *2 in. (5 cm)*
WHAT min size tank? *24 x 12 x 12 in. (60 x 30 x 30 cm)*

WHERE is it from? *Western Atlantic: from Puerto Rico and the Antilles to Curacao and Venezuela.*

Red-headed goby
Elacatinus puncticulatus

Another excellent fish for the nano-reef aquarium, this tiny species needs quiet companions, or it will seldom be seen— although it may well live out a hidden life feeding on small invertebrates from the live rock.

WHAT size? *1.5 in. (4 cm)*
WHAT min size tank? *18 x 12 x 12 in. (45 x 30 x 30 cm)*
WHERE is it from? *Eastern Pacific: Gulf of California to Ecuador.*

Coral gobies

PROFILE

The *Gobiodon* coral gobies, sometimes called clown gobies, are very appealing fishes, with their small size, stocky bodies, and bright colors. They are not the easiest of gobies to keep, but reward the fishkeeper who is prepared to provide the care they need by making fascinating inhabitants for suitable reef aquariums.

Coral gobies have toxic mucus that apparently is distasteful to other fishes, and this, plus their habit of living among the branches of stony corals, means that despite their small size they tend to avoid being eaten by predators. In the aquarium, they replicate their wild lifestyle of living among the branches of stony corals, and will often spawn, although raising the young appears to be extremely difficult. Their small size makes them appear to be ideal for the nano-reef aquarium, but growing their host corals in small tanks can be tricky.

WHERE do they live in the wild?
Typically found among the branches of *Acropora* and other ramified corals in shallow, often turbulent water.

WHAT aquarium environment?
Ideally, should be kept in a tank housing *Acropora* or other branching stony corals, although they will associate with soft corals. In aquariums without corals they tend to hide among rocks. A refugium can be useful to provide a supply of small live foods.

WHAT do they eat?
Usually eat dry or frozen foods provided they are of suitably small size; frozen copepods are particularly good, as these mimic the natural diet. Live brineshrimp or brineshrimp nauplii may sometimes be needed to get newly imported fishes to feed. Feed at least twice daily.

HOW hardy?
Not the hardiest of gobies: They are quite susceptible to white spot infections when stressed, and can sometimes be difficult to get feeding when first imported. The smaller species can easily get trapped in filter or pump intakes.

HOW compatible with other fishes?
Although *Gobiodon* species have toxic mucus that makes them distasteful to predators, they may be bullied by larger or more aggressive species, and if kept with more boisterous species they may be unable to compete for food. Several clown gobies can be kept in the same aquarium if plenty of branching

The neon blue stripes distinguish this fish from G. okinawae.

Citron goby
Gobiodon citrinus

A giant by Gobiodon *standards, the citron goby can be distinguished from the yellow coral goby (G. okinawae) by the neon blue stripes on the head and body, and its more extravagant fins. This is probably the most common aquarium import, and its larger size makes it a little easier to keep than some of its relatives—it can eat larger foods, and aquarium hardware poses less of a threat.*

WHAT size? *3 in. (7 cm)*
WHAT min size tank? *30 x 12 x 12 in. (75 x 30 x 30 cm)*
WHERE is it from? *From the Red Sea to the coast of Mozambique, east across the Indian Ocean and western Pacific to Samoa, north to southern Japan, south to the Great Barrier Reef.*

stony corals are present to provide habitat, and pairs can be formed by buying two individuals of the same species—*Gobiodon* gobies can change sex in both directions.

HOW compatible with invertebrates?

Completely harmless to invertebrates: When pairs spawn, they may damage their host coral slightly, but do no permanent harm.

WHAT do they cost?

★☆☆☆☆   ★★☆☆☆

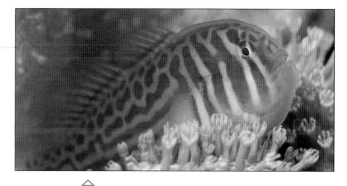

△

Green coral goby
Gobiodon histrio

Another very small species (although usually sold at slightly larger sizes than G. okinawae), this green-and-red goby makes a charming inhabitant for both nano-reefs and larger aquariums, provided that the habitat and tankmates are suitable.

WHAT size? 1.5 in. (4 cm)
WHAT min size tank? 18 x 12 x 12 in. (45 x 30 x 30 cm)
WHERE is it from? Red Sea, across the Indian Ocean and western Pacific as far east as Samoa, north to southern Japan, south to the Great Barrier Reef.

Yellow coral goby
Gobiodon okinawae

▷

This tiny, bright yellow goby is another common import for the aquarium trade, and is one of the smallest fishes that is regularly kept in the aquarium. Its small size means that it needs particular care with respect to choice of tankmates and providing a safe environment.

WHAT size? 1.5 in. (4 cm)
WHAT min size tank? 18 x 12 x 12 in. (45 x 30 x 30 cm)
WHERE is it from? Western Pacific Ocean: from southern Japan south to the Great Barrier Reef, east to the Marshall Islands.

Valenciennea species
Sleeper gobies

The *Valenciennea* gobies are large by the standards of the goby family. Although they are frequently imported and very popular, they can be quite difficult to keep, requiring specialized aquarium conditions (because of their method of feeding by sifting sand for small invertebrates) and careful selection of healthy individuals. Many of them are very attractive, and it is fascinating to watch them taking huge mouthfuls of sand and sifting it through their gill covers. However, their feeding activities can deplete sand beds of small creatures, and when added to established aquariums they may disturb huge quantities of detritus from the substrate, which may temporarily impact water quality.

WHERE do they live in the wild?
Usually found in lagoons and sandy or silty bays, living in pairs and usually staying close to their burrows. Some species can also be found over hard substrates.

WHAT aquarium environment?
Require large areas of open fine sand bed (preferably of live sand), which they sift constantly for food, as well as some live rock under which they can build burrows. An ideal tank layout would have most of the base of the tank as an open sand bed, with relatively little covered by live rock. Tall, slim live rock structures work well, and these can also be used to keep any corals well above the substrate, so they do not get covered in sand by feeding gobies.

WHAT do they eat?
Will eat most dry and frozen foods, but need their food to be presented close to the bottom of the tank.

HOW hardy?
Although otherwise generally hardy, these gobies often become very thin and waste away, despite apparently feeding well. This is thought to be the result of infestation with intestinal

parasites. It is possible to "worm" these fishes, but this requires a separate treatment tank and preparing food impregnated with a worming compound. However, a proportion of these gobies appear to be unaffected, and these usually do very well in the aquarium. For the best chance of getting one of these healthy individuals, choose a plump-looking fish in the dealer's tank, put a deposit on it, then leave it with the shop for two to three weeks. If it stays plump, it will probably do well; if it loses weight, it is likely to waste away.

HOW compatible with other fishes?
Generally peaceful with other fishes. Sleeper gobies live in male-female pairs, and are often

Blue-cheeked goby
◁ *Valenciennea strigata*

One of the most frequently imported sleeper gobies, this species is very attractive with its vivid yellow head with neon blue stripes, but requires a large aquarium and extensive areas of open sand bed.

WHAT size? *7 in. (18 cm)*
WHAT min size tank? *60 x 24 x 24 in. (150 x 60 x 60 cm)*
WHERE is it from? *Indian and western Pacific Oceans, from East Africa to Tuamoto, north to the Ryukyu Islands, south to New South Wales and Lord Howe Island.*

imported as such and can be kept together. May fight with other sleeper gobies (apart from their partners).

HOW
compatible with invertebrates?
When feeding may drop sand on corals; otherwise harmless.

WHAT do they cost?
★★☆☆☆   ★★★☆☆

Orange-spotted goby
Valenciennea puellaris

Another of the more colorful Valenciennea *species, the orange spotted goby is a common import, but like the blue-cheeked goby it is quite a large fish and needs a spacious aquarium.*

WHAT size? 8 in. (20 cm)
WHAT min size tank? 60 x 24 x 24 in. (150 x 60 x 60 cm)
WHERE is it from? Red Sea, across the Indian Ocean to the western Pacific, north to Ryukyu Islands, south to Great Barrier Reef and New Caledonia.

Ghost goby
Valenciennea sexguttata

One of the smaller sleeper gobies. This species is unusual in being almost completely white, apart from gold around the eye, pale blue spots on the head, and black spots in the dorsal fin. It requires similar care to the other Valenciennea *species.*

WHAT size? 5.5 in. (14 cm)
WHAT min size tank? 48 x 24 x 24 in. (120 x 60 x 60 cm)
WHERE is it from? Red Sea, Persian Gulf, and East African coast, across the Indian Ocean and western Pacific to Samoa, north to southern Japan, south to Queensland.

Dartfishes

▶ The dartfishes of the family Microdesmidae are often confused with gobies—in fact, many of them are routinely sold as gobies. Examples include the zebra dartfish *(Ptereleotris zebra)*, which in many aquarium shops is offered as a "shotsilk goby," or the various firefishes, which are often labeled fire gobies. Although they are related to the gobies (and in the past have been included among them), dartfishes lack some key goby features, such as fused pelvic fins. Dartfishes typically have better-developed swimbladders than gobies and tend to hover above the substrate rather than resting on it. The dartfishes as a whole are hardy, very peaceful fishes that pose no threat to invertebrates, so are ideal for the reef aquarium.

Price guide	
★	$24–32
★★	$32–40
★★★	$40–48
★★★★	$240–320

PROFILE

One small group of dartfishes are great favorites with marine aquarium enthusiasts. These are the firefishes, the three *Nemateleotris* species. All three are stunningly beautiful and fascinating to observe in the aquarium. However, be aware that they are the most likely of the dartfishes to jump out of the aquarium.

WHERE do they live in the wild?

Typically found on or at the base of reef slopes over rock, rubble, or sand seabeds, in areas swept by strong currents. Hover close to the substrate, sometimes in pairs or small groups, feeding on zooplankton and darting into holes when frightened. Depth range varies between species, from 20 to 230 ft. (6–70 m).

WHAT aquarium environment?

Like plenty of cover; plenty of live rock and invertebrates, with caves and crevices. Prefer strong currents. Species from deeper water prefer less bright light, especially when new to the aquarium. Do not need particularly large aquariums, as they tend to hover in one spot.

Nemateleotris species

Firefishes

WHAT do they eat?
Will eat small frozen crustaceans (copepods, brineshrimp, mysis) and fish roe, as well as most dry foods. Prefer food to be presented in midwater, although some learn to feed at the surface. Feed at least three times per day.

HOW hardy?
Generally very hardy, but prone to jumping out of the aquarium.

HOW compatible with other fishes?
Will not bother other fishes, and may be bullied or at least intimidated by large or boisterous companions. Should not be kept with their own kind (other than in mated pairs) except in very large tanks.

Firefish
Nemateleotris magnifica

This is the most widely available and least expensive of the firefishes, and it is typically found in shallower water than the others. It is no less beautiful, however, and its glowing red colors give the whole family their common name. The first dorsal fin ray in the other species is not nearly so large as in this species.

WHAT size? *3.5 in. (9 cm)*
WHAT min size tank? *36 x 18 x 18 in. (90 x 38 x 38 cm)*
WHERE is it from? *Indian and Pacific Oceans: from East Africa to Hawaii, Marquesas and Pitcairn Islands, north to Ryukyu Islands, south to New Caledonia.*

HOW compatible with invertebrates?
Harmless to all invertebrates.

WHAT do they cost?
★☆☆☆   ★★★★
N. helfrichi is the most expensive.

Nemateleotris species

Firefishes

Helfrich's firefish
Nemateleotris helfrichi

A dazzling deep-water gem, this species commands the highest price of any of the firefishes, and is far less frequently seen for sale than the other species. It is the least aggressive toward its own kind, and is also the smallest of the family. It prefers slightly subdued lighting.

WHAT size? *2.5 in. (6 cm)*
WHAT min size tank? *24 x 15 x 12 in. (60 x 38 x 30 cm)*
WHERE is it from? *Pacific Ocean: from Tuamoto Islands to Ryukyu Islands.*

Purple firefish
Nemateleotris decora

Found in deeper water than N. magnifica, *this stunning species is typically more expensive. It is the most assertive of the firefishes in the aquarium, being better able to cope with robust tankmates than its relatives.*

WHAT size? *3.5 in. (9 cm)*
WHAT min size tank? *36 x 15 x 15 in. (90 x 38 x 38 cm)*
WHERE is it from? *Indian and western Pacific Oceans: from Mauritius to Samoa, north to Ryukyu Islands, south to New Caledonia.*

Ptereleotris species

Dartfishes

PROFILE

These long, slender dartfishes are very hardy, peaceful, undemanding fishes, but with one exception—the zebra dartfish *(Ptereleotris zebra)*—they have not really enjoyed the popularity they deserve. Not so dazzling as the firefishes, they are still very attractive and are rather easier to keep than their more flamboyant cousins, being less prone to aerobatics and happy to live in groups of their own species or with other dartfishes.

WHERE do they live in the wild?
Typically over rubble or sandy seabeds, on outer reef slopes swept by strong currents, but sometimes in lagoons, at depths ranging from 16.5–165 ft. (5–50 m). Found in pairs or small or large groups, depending on species, typically close to the seabed. Most species dart into burrows when alarmed.

WHAT aquarium environment?
Like some live rock and invertebrates for cover, and a sand bed for building burrows—they like to dig under the edges of rocks. Prefer strong currents and need a reasonable amount of open water. Deep-water species prefer relatively low light levels.

WHAT do they eat?
Will eat any dry or frozen food of suitable size. Feed at least three times a day.

HOW hardy?
Generally hardy and disease resistant. May jump out of uncovered tanks, or into overflow chambers.

HOW compatible with other fishes?
Peaceful with other species and can usually be kept with others of their own kind, or in mixed groups of different *Ptereleotris* species. Prefer quiet companions: may hide constantly if kept with aggressive species.

HOW compatible with invertebrates?
Harmless to all invertebrates.

WHAT do they cost?
★☆☆☆ ★★★☆

Zebra dartfish
Ptereleotris zebra

The most popular of the dartfishes, this species has a complex, subtle color scheme that rewards close inspection. When kept in groups in the aquarium, pairs will often form, and will lay clutches of eggs in caves and crevices in the rocks.

WHAT size? 5 in. (12 cm)
WHAT min size tank? 48 x 18 x 15 in. (120 x 45 x 38 m)
WHERE is it from? Red Sea, western Indian Ocean to Line Islands and Marquesas in the Pacific, north to Ryukyu Islands, south to Great Barrier Reef, also Marianas and Marshall Islands.

Ptereleotris species

Dartfishes

Striped dartfish
Ptereleotris grammistes

A stunningly beautiful species, this is a deep-water fish that prefers plenty of hiding places, subdued lighting, and quiet companions; otherwise it tends to be very shy and have trouble adapting to the aquarium.

WHAT size? 4 in. (10 cm)
WHAT min size tank? 48 x 18 x 15 in. (120 x 45 x 38 cm)
WHERE is it from? Indian Ocean and west Pacific Ocean: from Mauritius and the Maldives to the Solomon Islands, north to the Ryukyu Islands, south to the Great Barrier Reef.

Scissortail dartfish
Ptereleotris evides

Apart from P. zebra, this species, with its flamboyant velvety black fins and bright blue eyes, is the most commonly imported dartfish. It is an excellent reef aquarium fish, bolder than many other Ptereleotris species.

WHAT size? 5.5 in. (14 cm)
WHAT min size tank? 48 x 18 x 18 in. (120 x 45 x 45 cm)
WHERE is it from? Red Sea, Indian and Pacific Oceans, from East Africa to Line Islands and Society Islands, north to Ryukyu Islands, south to Lord Howe Island.

Blue dartfish
Ptereleotris monoptera

This lovely metallic blue to green species (the color is variable) is an occasional import. Although not common, it is easy to keep and makes a fine addition to a reef aquarium with other peaceful fishes.

WHAT size? *5.5 in. (12 cm)*
WHAT min size tank? *48 x 18 x 15 in. (120 x 45 x 38 cm)*
WHERE is it from? *The Seychelles and Chagos Islands in the Indian Ocean, to the western Pacific Ocean.*

Black-tail dartfish
Ptereleotris heteroptera

This species is one of several dartfishes that look similar, long and slim, colored in shimmering pale metallic blue—it can be distinguished from others by the black spot at the tail. Care is similar for all of these species, so any misidentification doesn't cause any practical problems.

WHAT size? *5.5 in. (14 cm)*
WHAT min size tank? *48 x 18 x 18 in. (120 x 45 x 45 cm)*
WHERE is it from? *Red Sea, Indian and Pacific oceans, from East Africa to Marianas, Caroline Islands, Marshall Islands, Line Islands, Marquesas, and Society Islands, north to Ryukyu Islands, south to Lord Howe Island.*

Blennies

▷ Blennies as a family may be more redolent of the rockpool than the coral reef to the layman, but for the marine aquarium enthusiast they offer a number of desirable species. The blennies commonly kept in the aquarium divide into two categories: herbivores and carnivores. The former rasp algae from hard substrates—hair algae in some species, microalgae in others—and are not always completely safe with invertebrates, as they may sometimes extend their grazing activities to some corals and to clam mantles. The carnivorous blennies prey on zooplankton and small crustaceans living on live rock and in sand beds, and are generally a safer bet in a reef aquarium than their algae-eating cousins.

Price guide

★	$24–32
★★	$32–40
★★★	$40–48
★★★★	$64–80

PROFILE

Most of the *Ecsenius* blennies are herbivores, feeding by grazing microalgae from rocks, although the most frequently kept species is atypical in that it is primarily a planktivore. This is the midas blenny *(Ecsenius midas)*, which is also the only one of the *Ecsenius* blennies that can be considered truly safe with all invertebrates; the herbivorous species may occasionally eat or damage particular corals. However, they are fascinating fishes to keep, and some of the smaller species are among the few algae grazers that are small enough to keep in nano-reef aquariums.

WHERE do they live in the wild?

Found only in areas of dense coral growth, usually in shallow water, including reef crests and tide pools, as well as in lagoons. Live in small holes or crevices, venturing out to graze algae, or in the case of *Ecsenius midas,* to swim among shoals of *Pseudanthias* species and feed on plankton.

WHAT aquarium environment?

Appreciate plenty of live rock to provide both holes and crevices to use as homes, and grazing opportunities.

Ecsenius blennies

WHAT do they eat?
Will eat most aquarium foods, but should be provided with some algae-based products, and herbivorous species graze algae growing on the live rock and aquarium glass. Feed at least twice daily.

HOW hardy?
Usually hardy, but may jump out of open aquariums.

HOW compatible with other fishes?
May be territorial toward their own and related species, and may show aggression toward small gobies and similar fishes.

HOW compatible with invertebrates?
Only the midas blenny (*Ecsenius midas*) can be considered to be safe with all invertebrates. The herbivorous species may occasionally eat certain corals or scrape the mantles of tridacnid clams.

WHAT do they cost?
★☆☆☆ ★★★★
E. bicolor and *E. pictus* are the least expensive (★); *E. gravieri* the most expensive (★★★★).

▲ *The midas blenny is a long, slender fish, its shape and color helping it blend in with shoals of Pseudanthias species.*

Midas blenny
Ecsenius midas

This long, slender fish can become a real pet in the aquarium, and its antics will keep the fishkeeper well entertained. Unlike others in this genus it is primarily planktivorous, and its diet should reflect this. In the wild it swims among shoals of Pseudanthias species, its coloration allowing it to blend in with them.

WHAT size? 5 in. (13 cm)
WHAT min size tank? 48 x 18 x 15 in. (120 x 45 x 38 cm)
WHERE is it from? Red Sea, across the Indian and western Pacific oceans from East Africa to the Marquesas.

◀ *A midas blenny in typical pose, peeking out of a hole in the rocks.*

Ecsenius species

Ecsenius blennies

◁ Bicolor blenny
Ecsenius bicolor

This species has several color phases, but only the most common, the orange and purple-brown form, is frequently offered for sale. Although safe with most invertebrates, it may bite large-polyp stony corals and the mantles of giant clams.

WHAT size? *4.5 in. (11 cm)*
WHAT min size tank? *36 x 18 x 15 in. (90 x 45 x 38 cm)*
WHERE is it from? *Indian and western Pacific oceans: from the Maldives to Micronesia, north to the Ryukyu Islands and south to the Great Barrier Reef.*

Red Sea mimic blenny ▷
Ecsenius gravieri

This is a very beautiful species but it tends to be expensive. It is a mimic of the venomous blackline blenny (Meiacanthus nigrolineatus). Most invertebrates are usually safe with this species, but it has been reported to eat the tissue of small-polyp stony corals.

WHAT size? *3 in. (8 cm)*
WHAT min size tank? *36 x 15 x 15 in. (90 x 38 x 38 cm)*
WHERE is it from? *Red Sea.*

Tail-spot blenny
Ecsenius stigmatura

A very distinctive little blenny (the combination of the tail spot and stripe on the face is unique), this species is usually safe with corals and is a good algae grazer for a nano-reef aquarium.

WHAT size? *2.5 in. (6 cm)*
WHAT min tank? *24 x 12 x 12 in. (60 x 30 x 30 cm)*
WHERE is it from? *Western central Pacific Ocean: the Philippines and Indonesia.*

▶ *The tail-spot blenny is typical of several small herbivorous* Ecsenius *blennies.*

Painted blenny
Ecsenius pictus

This intricately patterned little species makes a great addition to the nano-reef aquarium, although it can be quite territorial, so it requires robust, if not large, companions.

WHAT size? *2 in. (5 cm)*
WHAT min size tank? *24 x 12 x 12 in. (60 x 30 x 30 cm)*
WHERE is it from? *Western central Pacific Ocean: the Philippines, Indonesia, and the Solomon Islands.*

Blenniella chrysospilos

Red flymo

This colorful species is very entertaining to watch as it grazes algae and detritus from live rock in the aquarium, hopping from place to place. It needs to be kept in a well-established aquarium with plenty of microalgae growth and detritus, as, like some other herbivorous blennies, it can have problems adapting to aquarium foods.

WHAT size?
5 in. (13 cm)

WHERE is it from?
Indian and western Pacific oceans: East Africa to the Society Islands, north to the Ryukyu Islands.

WHERE does it live in the wild?
On reef flats, often in surge-exposed areas.

WHAT aquarium environment?
Needs plenty of live rock to provide grazing opportunities and shelter.

WHAT minimum size tank? 48 x 18 x 15 in. (120 x 45 x 38 cm)

WHAT does it eat?
Grazes microalgae from live rock and the aquarium glass; will also eat dried seaweed sheets and flakes.

▲ Flymo blennies are cute, but need plenty of algae to graze on.

HOW hardy?
Reasonably hardy, provided it gets enough food.

HOW compatible with other fishes?
Generally ignores unrelated species, but should not be kept with its own kind.

HOW compatible with invertebrates?
Usually safe, but may occasionally nip stony corals or clam mantles.

WHAT does it cost?
★★☆☆

Salarias fasciatus

Algae blenny

PROFILE

This species looks exactly as most people would imagine a blenny—every inch the rockpool dweller, or so it seems. In reality, it lives on coral reefs. This blenny should ideally be kept in an aquarium with a good supply of algae, as initially it can be difficult to get it to feed on prepared foods.

WHAT size?
5.5 in. (14 cm)

WHERE is it from?
Red Sea, Indian Ocean, and western Pacific Ocean: from East Africa to Samoa, north to the Ryukyu Islands, south to the Great Barrier Reef.

WHERE does it live in the wild?
On reef flats, in shallow lagoons, estuaries, and seaward reefs. Usually in shallow water, in areas of mixed coral, rubble, and sand.

WHAT aquarium environment?
Needs plenty of live rock to provide grazing opportunities; ideally a good supply of algae should be available.

WHAT minimum size tank?
24 x 18 x 18 in. (120 x 45 x 45 cm)

WHAT does it eat?
Needs an algae-based diet: Dried seaweed sheets and flakes, spirulina-based dry foods may be accepted, but the ideal is to have a good growth of filamentous algae present in the aquarium.

HOW hardy?
Reasonably hardy provided that it has enough algae to eat.

HOW compatible with other fishes?
Can be aggressive toward other fishes; needs robust tankmates.

HOW compatible with invertebrates?
Usually safe but may occasionally rasp at clam mantles and some stony corals.

WHAT does it cost?
★★☆☆

▼ *Although not brightly colored, the algae blenny is an attractive and interesting fish.*

Meiacanthus species

Fang blennies

PROFILE

These slender, elegant blennies are very beautiful and near-perfect fishes for the reef aquarium. The *Meiacanthus* blennies are unusual among their family in two ways. First, they have well-developed swimbladders, and so can hover effortlessly in midwater and swim with an ease that contrasts sharply with the labored movement of most of their relatives. Second, they have a venomous bite that serves to deter predators. As a result, they are mimicked by other, harmless, species that in consequence enjoy the same protection. It is wise to avoid handling these blennies, and to be aware of where they are when working in the aquarium. However, they are not aggressive; their bite has been compared to a bee sting.

The only difficulty in keeping *Meiacanthus* blennies is ensuring that they get enough to eat. Most species are quite slow feeders—they identify a prey organism, such as a small crustacean on the substrate, hover over it, and curl their bodies before finally striking. They usually accept frozen foods, but have difficulty competing with faster, more decisive feeders. Keeping them in an aquarium with lots of live rock to provide plenty of small organisms can be of benefit, as can a refugium. Those species that feed more

on plankton in open water, most notably the striped fang blenny *(Meiacanthus grammistes),* are easier in this respect.

WHERE do they live in the wild?
In lagoons and on seaward reefs; some found over coral rubble beds, others around drop-offs. Range from shallow water to around 100 ft. (30 m) deep, depending on species.

WHAT aquarium environment?
Prefer extensive areas of live rock to provide both cover and hunting opportunities. A refugium can also be useful as a source of small live foods.

WHAT do they eat?
Will usually eat small frozen crustaceans, such as brineshrimp and copepods, and will

Yellowtail fang blenny
Meiacanthus atrodorsalis

A lovely fish, but not particularly common in the aquarium trade. This species, with its long flowing tail fin, is a more than typically elegant Meiacanthus *blenny.*

WHAT size? 4.5 in. (11 cm)
WHAT min size tank? 48 x 18 x 15 in. (120 x 45 x 38 cm)
WHERE is it from? Western Pacific Ocean: from Bali and the Philippines to Samoa, throughout Micronesia, north to the Ryukyu Islands, and south to the Great Barrier Reef and New Caledonia.

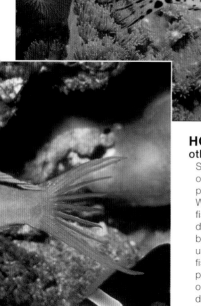

HOW compatible with other fishes?

Should not be kept with their own kind, except in mated pairs or groups in large tanks. Will not usually bother other fishes, and their poisonous bite deters most other fishes from bothering them; they are not usually intimidated by larger fishes. However, most species, particularly those that hunt prey on the substrate, are slow and deliberate feeders and may have trouble competing for food with fast-moving or boisterous tankmates, so quiet companions are best.

HOW compatible with invertebrates?

Completely safe with all invertebrates.

WHAT do they cost?

★☆☆☆　★★★☆

sometimes learn to accept flake foods. Also hunt small crustaceans on the substrate. Feed at least twice daily.

HOW hardy?

Fang blennies are usually reasonably hardy, provided that they get enough to eat.

Striped fang blenny
Meiacanthus grammistes

The most commonly sold of the fang blennies, this species is bolder and spends more of its time hovering in open water than most of its relatives, which tend to stay closer to the substrate. It is a very attractive species, with metallic gold highlighting around the head overlaying the black-and-white stripes.

WHAT size? 4.5 in. (11 cm)
WHAT min size tank? 48 x 18 x 15 in. (120 x 45 x 38 cm)
WHERE is it from? Western Pacific Ocean: from Indochina to Papua New Guinea, the Great Barrier Reef, and the Ryukyu Islands.

Meiacanthus species

Fang blennies

Mozambique fang blenny
Meiacanthus mossambicus

This blenny, with its unusual gray, green, and yellow color scheme, is one of the hardiest Meiacanthus *species, but ideally it should be kept with relatively quiet companions.*

WHAT size? *4 in. (10 cm)*
WHAT min size tank? *48 x 18 x 15 in. (120 x 45 x 38 cm)*
WHERE is it from? *Western Indian Ocean: East Africa, the Comoros, and Madagascar.*

Blackline fang blenny
Meiacanthus nigrolineatus

This beautiful blenny is similar to Meiacanthus atrodorsalis *in color, but can be distinguished by the black stripes in the dorsal fin and along the upper flanks. As a Red Sea endemic species, it is expensive.*

WHAT size? *3.5 in. (8.5 cm)*
WHAT min size tank? *48 x 18 x 15 in. (120 x 45 x 38 cm)*
WHERE is it from? *Red Sea and Gulf of Aden.*

Smith's fang blenny
Meiacanthus smithi ▷

Subtly attractive rather than gaudy, this is one of the smaller Meiacanthus species and is quite frequently seen for sale. The tail fin is characteristically less lyre-shaped than in other fang blennies.

WHAT size? *3.5 in. (8.5 cm)*
WHAT min size tank? *48 x 18 x 15 in. (120 x 45 x 38 cm)*
WHERE is it from? *Eastern Indian Ocean and western Pacific Ocean: Sri Lanka to Java.*

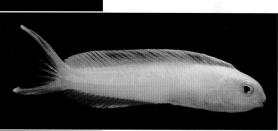

Canary blenny
◁ ### *Meiacanthus oulanensis*

This beautiful all-yellow species, with its flowing lyre-shaped tail, makes a superb addition to a reef aquarium. It tends to be more expensive than some other Meiacanthus *blennies because of its restricted geographical range in the wild.*

WHAT size? *4.5 in. (11 cm)*
WHAT min size tank? *48 x 18 x 15 in. (120 x 45 x 38 cm)*
WHERE is it from? *Western central Pacific Ocean: Fiji.*

Hawkfishes

▷ The hawkfishes are a family of predatory fishes that really earn their common name. They spend most of their time perching on rocks or corals, watching for prey (usually crustaceans or small fishes), then darting out to catch their victims. Their swimbladders are poorly developed, so they do not swim well—they sink if they stop moving.

As a rule they are extremely hardy, and the only real threat to their health is jumping out of the aquarium. Unusually, this is often not the result of being startled, or being chased by their tankmates, but because they jump in pursuit of insects flying over the aquarium.

Price guide

★	$32–48
★★	$48–72

PROFILE

As a rule, in the aquarium hawkfishes are highly entertaining and very endearing fishes that rapidly become great pets. They are intelligent little fishes and quickly learn to recognize their keepers. They have keen eyesight and often seem to be watching events outside the aquarium as much as inside it.

WHERE do they live in the wild?

Perch among corals or rocks in current-swept areas, darting out to capture prey—either crustaceans or small fishes. Usually found singly. Depth range varies by species, from 3 to 150 ft. (1–45 m).

WHAT aquarium environment?

Like to have plenty of live rock and corals on which they can perch to look out for prey.

WHAT do they eat?

Will eat most frozen and dry foods; larger frozen crustaceans such as mysis and krill are ideal, and larger specimens will also relish fresh or frozen shrimp from the fishmonger or chopped white-fish flesh. Color-enhancing dry foods are also useful in preventing color loss.

Hawkfishes

HOW hardy?

Hawkfishes are generally extremely hardy and disease resistant. They have been known to survive disease outbreaks that wipe out every other fish in their tanks. They sometimes jump from open aquariums.

HOW compatible with other fishes?

Will not usually tolerate other members of their own species, except in very large aquariums or if bought as mated pairs. Most are quite aggressive and are best kept with larger or similarly robust tankmates. They will eat any fishes small enough to fit into their mouths.

HOW compatible with invertebrates?

Completely safe with corals and clams but may eat shrimps and occasionally small snails. Smaller species pose less of a threat than larger ones.

WHAT do they cost?

See individual entries.

Flame hawkfish
Neocirrhites armatus

With probably the most intensely red color of any aquarium fish, this is one of the best hawkfishes for the reef aquarium. In the wild it lives among stony coral heads, often in very shallow water, and is ideal for a reef aquarium focused on small-polyp stony corals, such as Acropora *species.*

WHAT size? 3.5 in. (9 cm)
WHAT min size tank? 36 x 18 x 15 in. (90 x 45 x 38 cm)
WHERE is it from? Pacific Ocean from the Ryukyu Islands to Marianas, Caroline Islands, Wake Islands, and south to the Great Barrier Reef.
WHAT does it cost? ★★

Amblycirrhitus, Cirrhitichthys, Oxycirrhitus species

Hawkfishes

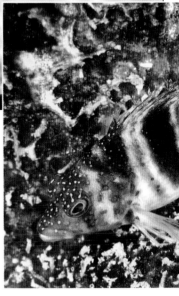

Pixie hawkfish
Cirrhitichthys oxycephalus

*This species is typical of the
Cirrhitichthys hawkfishes. Like the
other Cirrhitichthys species, it has
attractive tassels at the tips of its
spiny front dorsal fin rays. Once
established in the aquarium, it may
become aggressive toward newly
introduced fishes, particularly quiet,
passive species, so it is best kept
with larger or bolder tankmates.*

WHAT size? *4 in. (10 cm)*
WHAT min size tank? *36 x 18 x
15 in. (90 x 45 x 38 cm)*
WHERE is it from? *Red Sea, Indian
and Pacific Oceans, from East Africa
to the Marquesas, the Galapagos,
and the Gulf of California, north to
the Marianas, south to New
Caledonia.*
WHAT does it cost? ★☆

Red-spotted hawkfish
Amblycirrhitus pinos

This species is unusual among aquarium hawkfishes in that it comes from the tropical Atlantic— most other hawkfishes are Pacific or Indian Ocean species. In the aquarium, like other hawkfishes it makes a great pet but its predatory nature means that tankmates must be chosen with care.

WHAT size? 4 in. (10 cm)
WHAT min size tank? 36 x 18 x 15 in. (90 x 45 x 38 cm)
WHERE is it from? Western Atlantic Ocean: from southern Florida and Texas, the Bahamas, and the Caribbean Sea to Brazil. Also reported from St. Helena in the eastern Atlantic.
WHAT does it cost? ★☆

Longnose hawkfish
Oxycirrhitus typus

This species is a longtime favorite for its unusual shape and striking red-and-white checked pattern. In the wild it lives in quite deep water, perching among the branches of gorgonians, and it prefers slightly subdued lighting. It has a large mouth so should not be kept with very small tankmates.

WHAT size? 5 in. (13 cm)
WHAT min size tank? 48 x 18 x 18 in. (120 x 45 x 45 cm)
WHERE is it from? Red Sea, Indian and Pacific Oceans, from East Africa to Hawaii, the Galapagos, and the Gulf of California, north to southern Japan, south to New Caledonia.
WHAT does it cost? ★★

Cardinalfishes

▶ With one exception (the Banggai cardinalfish) this family tends to be rather underrated by fishkeepers. This is unfortunate, as they are very attractive, peaceful, hardy, and usually gregarious fishes that look very good in a shoal in a reef aquarium. Most do not grow very large, and so are easy to accommodate in even modestly sized aquariums. Many cardinals spawn regularly in the aquarium, and at least some species are mouthbrooders, the males holding the eggs until they hatch. Some species are crepuscular or nocturnal, but in the aquarium they quickly get used to being more active during the day, especially if the tank has shady areas.

Price guide	
★	$16–24
★★	$24–32
★★★	$40–48
★★★★	$48–64

PROFILE

Many cardinals are very abundant in the wild, often found in very large shoals, although one species—the Banggai cardinal—has a very restricted range and fishkeepers should look for tank-bred examples. In general, cardinals are not as popular as they should be, given their many virtues.

WHERE do they live in the wild?
In lagoons and on reefs, in coral-rich areas, usually in shallow water, generally in small or large schools, feeding on zooplankton. Some species shelter among the spines of large sea urchins.

WHAT aquarium environment?
Need plenty of live rock, arranged into caves and overhangs, and invertebrates to provide cover.

WHAT do they eat?
Most frozen and dry foods. Feed at least twice daily.

HOW hardy?
Most cardinals are very hardy and disease resistant.

HOW compatible with other fishes?
Many cardinals will live in groups with others of their own kind or in pairs, although all individuals should be added

Cardinalfishes

to the aquarium together. Not usually aggressive toward other species, although the female partners of mouthbrooding males will chase off fishes that come too close. May be picked on by aggressive tankmates, so quieter fishes make better companions.

HOW compatible with invertebrates?

Safe with corals and clams, and with most other invertebrates. Larger cardinals occasionally eat very small shrimps.

WHAT do they cost?

Z. leptacanthus is the least expensive (★); *P. kauderni* the most expensive (★★★★).

Banggai cardinal
Pterapogon kauderni

This species is the only one of the cardinals that is very popular with fishkeepers — it has been very fashionable for several years. Unfortunately, it has a very limited range in the wild and collection for the aquarium trade is threatening the wild population. This is ironic, because this species is very easy to breed in captivity — it is a mouthbrooder. If buying this

species, always buy tank-bred fishes. It is less sociable than most other cardinals and should be kept singly or in mated pairs, except in very large aquariums.

WHAT size? *3 in. (8 cm)*
WHAT min size tank? *36 x 18 x 15 in. (90 x 45 x 38 cm)*
WHERE is it from? *Western central Pacific Ocean: found only around the Banggai Islands, Indonesia.*

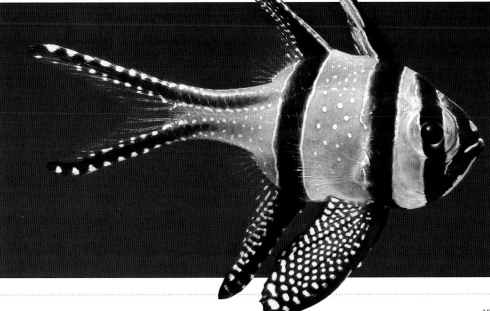

Apogon, Sphaeramia, Zoramia species

Cardinalfishes

Yellow-striped cardinal
Apogon cyanosoma

This attractive yellow-orange striped species is one of the more regularly imported cardinals. It can be kept singly, in pairs or in groups (preferably of five or more) and has all the cardinalfish virtues of hardiness, a peaceable nature, and being harmless to all invertebrates, with the possible exception of very small shrimps.

WHAT size? *3 in. (8 cm)*
WHAT min size tank? *36 x 15 x 15 in. (90 x 38 x 38 cm)*
WHERE is it from? *Red Sea and Indian and western Pacific Oceans, from East Africa to Fiji, north to Ryukyu Islands, south to New Caledonia.*

Pajama cardinal
Sphaeramia nematoptera

This very unusually patterned species is extremely hardy, peaceful, and an excellent choice for the reef aquarium. It is a mouthbrooder and often spawns in the aquarium—pairs will often form when small groups are kept together.

WHAT size? *3.5 in. (8.5 cm)*
WHAT min size tank? *60 x 18 x 15 in. (90 x 45 x 38 cm)*
WHERE is it from? *Western Pacific Ocean, from Java to Fiji and Tonga, north to Ryukyu Islands, south to Great Barrier Reef.*

Bluestreak cardinal
Zoramia leptacanthus

This species is representative of several similar species: They are all very small and silvery to almost transparent with metallic blue markings. They are excellent species to keep in small or even large groups, depending on aquarium size. The genus Zoramia was previously included in Apogon.

WHAT size? *2.5 in. (6 cm)*
WHAT min size tank? *24 x 12 x 12 in. (60 x 30 x 30 cm)*
WHERE is it from? *Red Sea and Indian and western Pacific oceans, from East Africa to Samoa and Tonga, north to Ryukyu Islands, south to New Caledonia.*

Yellow cardinal
Apogon seali

This species is slightly larger than many other cardinalfishes. It is a relatively uncommon import, but very attractive and straightforward to keep, like others in the family.

WHAT size? *4 in. (10 cm)*
WHAT min size tank? *36 x 18 x 18 in. (90 x 45 x 45 cm)*
WHERE is it from? *Western Pacific Ocean: from Malaysia to the Solomon Islands, north to southern Japan, south to Western Australia.*

Tilefishes

▶ The tilefishes are fascinating, beautiful fishes, but are not easy to keep, as they have some very specific requirements, and should ideally have an aquarium designed specifically for them. They may also struggle to adapt to aquarium foods—it is wise to ask to see them feeding before buying. They are very much fishes for expert fishkeepers who are willing to provide the special care they require.

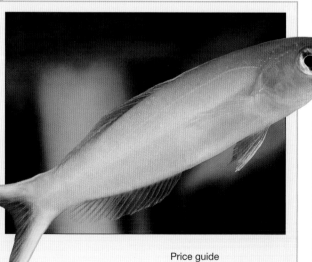

Price guide

★	$48–64
★★	$64–80
★★★	$128–192

PROFILE

Some tilefishes have dazzling colors, others can change their colors at astounding speeds, and all of them make very interesting aquarium inhabitants—but they are not fishes that fit readily into the typical reef tank. They can be very rewarding for those aquarists prepared to meet their special requirements.

WHERE do they live in the wild?

Over sand or rubble seabeds at the bases of reef slopes, in pairs or groups feeding on zooplankton. Some species build large mounds of coral rubble to house their burrows. Found at depths of 60–275 ft. (18–80 m).

WHAT aquarium environment?

Require plenty of swimming space and wide expanses of open substrate. Need larger tanks than their size would suggest, as they are highly active. Strong currents are preferred. It is best to set up a special tank designed around their needs, with well-separated live rock structures, wide areas of deep sand and rubble bed, and powerful circulation pumps. Prefer slightly subdued lighting.

WHAT do they eat?

Frozen crustaceans (mysis, brineshrimp, krill, copepods)

and fish roe. May sometimes require feeding with live brineshrimp when first added to the aquarium. Feed at least three times a day.

HOW hardy?

May have difficulty adapting to the aquarium if conditions are not appropriate or aggressive fishes are present. May have swimbladder problems resulting from improper decompression — avoid buying fishes that cannot maintain their position in the water or that swim in odd postures. May jump from open aquariums, and if startled may crash into the sides of the aquarium.

HOW compatible with other fishes?

Peaceful with other fishes. Best kept in pairs or small groups with their own species or in mixed groups of tilefishes — they tend to adapt better to aquarium life if not on their own. Should not be kept with boisterous tankmates; other peaceful, quiet fishes make good companions.

HOW compatible with invertebrates?

Usually safe with all invertebrates except for very small shrimps.

WHAT do they cost?

See individual entries.

Purple tilefish
Hoplolatilus purpureus

This stunningly beautiful species is the most commonly imported tilefish. It is often offered in mated pairs, and this is the ideal way to buy this fish.

WHAT size? *5 in. (13 cm)*
WHAT min size tank? *48 x 24 x 24 in. (120 x 60 x 60 cm)*
WHERE is it from? *Western central Pacific Ocean: the Philippines and Solomon Islands.*
WHAT does it cost? ★★

Tilefishes

Hoplolatilus species

Flashing tilefish
Hoplolatilus chlupatyi

This species can vary its colors at astonishing speed—hence its common name. It is rarely available and tends to be expensive.

WHAT size? *5 in. (13 cm)*
WHAT min size tank? *48 x 24 x 24 in. (120 x 60 x 60 cm)*
WHERE is it from? *Western central Pacific Ocean: the Philippines.*
WHAT does it cost? ★★★

Bluehead tilefish
Hoplolatilus starcki

The very distinctive bluehead tilefish requires similar care to other tilefishes, but has a stronger preference for subdued lighting.

WHAT size? *6 in. (15 cm)*
WHAT min size tank? *60 x 24 x 24 in. (150 x 60 x 60 cm)*
WHERE is it from? *Western Pacific Ocean: from Moluccas and the Philippines to Timor, Marianas, New Caledonia, and Pitcairn Island.*
WHAT does it cost? ★★

Skunk tilefish
Hoplolatilus marcosi

Regarded as slightly hardier than most tilefishes, this is one of the more common species in the aquarium trade. In the wild it builds large rubble mounds.

▲ Like others of the family, the skunk tilefish is best kept with others of its own species.

WHAT size? 5 in. (12 cm)
WHAT min size tank? 48 x 24 x 24 in. (120 x 60 x 60 cm)
WHERE is it from? Western central Pacific Ocean: Indonesia, Palau, Papua New Guinea, the Philippines, and Solomon Islands.
WHAT does it cost? ★☆ ★★

▶ The skunk tilefish's blunt head is well adapted for burrowing.

Angelfishes

▶ The angelfish family (Pomacanthidae) includes some of the most beautiful marine fishes, many of which are long-established favorites with fishkeepers. Unfortunately, however, many angelfishes are difficult to keep, with nutritional problems, disease susceptibility, territorial behavior, and, in some cases, sheer size posing significant challenges.

For the reef aquarium keeper, things are even more complicated when it comes to angelfishes. Most angelfishes are grazers of algae and sessile invertebrates. Although the favored food of most grazing angels is sponges, few of them will pass up the chance to eat, or at least sample, other sessile invertebrates, such as corals and clams. This obviously tends to limit the possibilities for keeping angelfishes in the reef aquarium, particularly when combined with some of the other difficulties.

Price guide

★	$32–48
★★	$48–72
★★★	$80–96
★★★★	$96–128
★★★★★	$128–240

This is ironic, as the typical reef aquarium environment, with high water quality and an abundance of live rock, is much more congenial to most angels (and in particular to some of the more difficult

◄ *Angelfishes are often very beautiful, but are not always easy to keep in the reef aquarium.*

of very atypical angels that instead of grazing on sessile invertebrates hunt plankton in the water column. These are very good fishes for the reef aquarium.

Other angels, both the small *Centropyge* species and the larger angels, need to be added with caution to the reef aquarium, choosing species carefully and restricting the range of sessile invertebrates that are kept with them. Some of the larger angels are proving to be less destructive in the reef aquarium than was originally thought, although experience is still relatively limited. The situation with *Centropyge* angels is the opposite: These fishes were for a long time considered to be safe in the reef aquarium, but extensive experience has actually shown that this is far from being the case. However, some of them can make good reef tank fishes in suitable circumstances.

species) than the traditional fish-only aquarium. In fact, the best aquarium environment for most angelfishes is probably a fish-only tank run as if it were a reef system, using live rock for filtration and decoration.

However, this does not mean that it is not possible to keep angelfishes in the reef aquarium. One genus, *Genicanthus,* is made up

Genicanthus species

Swallowtail angels

The swallowtail angels (*Genicanthus* species) are by far the best angelfishes for the reef aquarium. They feed primarily on plankton and will almost always leave sessile invertebrates such as corals and clams alone. They are also unusual among angelfishes in that they show very obvious differences in appearance between the sexes. They begin life as females, with some individuals (presumably dominant ones within a group) subsequently transforming into males. Remarkably, at least in some species, males kept without females have reverted to female coloration.

WHERE do they live in the wild?

Most species are found in groups, usually with one male and several females, typically in rocky areas or around coral reefs, often on steep slopes and drop-offs. Many *Genicanthus* angels range into deep water, some to over 330 ft. (100 m) depth.

WHAT aquarium environment?

Plenty of open water, plus some caves and crevices for shelter. Those collected in deep water prefer subdued illumination initially, but will usually adapt to brighter lighting.

WHAT do they eat?

Readily accept most frozen foods of suitable size; frozen crustaceans (mysis, brineshrimp, krill, copepods) and fish and lobster roe are ideal. Will usually adapt to eating dry foods. Should be fed at least twice daily.

HOW hardy?

Generally hardy and easy to keep, provided that they do not have swimbladder problems resulting from poor collection techniques.

HOW compatible with other fishes?

Females can be kept in groups with or without a male, but only one male of a species should be kept per tank. Swallowtail angels generally ignore unrelated fishes, but occasionally chase smaller planktivorous species. Any territoriality is usually reduced in larger aquariums.

HOW compatible with invertebrates?

Almost always safe with all invertebrates. Swallowtail angels very seldom bother corals or clams, and other invertebrates are not at risk, as these angels have small mouths for their size. Very occasionally some individuals will pick at specific corals, but this is highly unusual.

WHAT do they cost?

★☆☆☆☆ ★★★★★

▲ The female bellus angel is a beautiful fish, and a perfect angel for the reef aquarium.

◄ Male bellus angels are relatively drably colored, compared with the female.

▶ This species is occasionally sold as a vampire angel, because of the fanglike marks on the mouth.

Bellus angel
Genicanthus bellus

This species is somewhat unusual in that the female is more attractive than the male. It is one of the hardiest of the Genicanthus angels, as well as one of the most beautiful, and a great addition to a medium-sized or large reef aquarium.

WHAT size? 7 in. (18 cm)
WHAT min size tank? 48 x 24 x 24 in. (120 x 60 x 60 cm)
WHERE is it from? Cocos-Keeling Atoll in the Indian Ocean, the Philippines, Guam, Palau, Cook Islands, Society Islands, and Tonga in the Pacific Ocean.

Swallowtail angels

Red Sea swallowtail angel
Genicanthus caudovittatus

This fairly expensive species is similar in coloration (in both males and females) to G. melanospilos from the Pacific. It is quite often sold in pairs.

WHAT size? *8 in. (20 cm)*
WHAT min size tank? *60 x 24 x 24 in. (150 x 60 x 60 cm)*
WHERE is it from? *Red Sea and western Indian Ocean (East African coast, Maldives, Madagascar, Reunion, Mauritius).*

Blackspot angel
Genicanthus melanospilos

This is one of the most widely available and inexpensive of these angels; it is often available in male-female pairs—the difference between the sexes is very dramatic.
▽

▼ *The male blackspot angel has a striped pattern also seen in the related Red Sea and Japanese swallowtail angels.*

WHAT size? *7 in. (18 cm)*
WHAT min size tank? *48 x 24 x 24 in. (120 x 60 x 60 cm)*
WHERE is it from? *Wide range across the western Pacific Ocean, from Indonesia north to Ryukyu Islands, south and east to Tonga.*

▼ *The female blackspot angel looks very different from the male.*

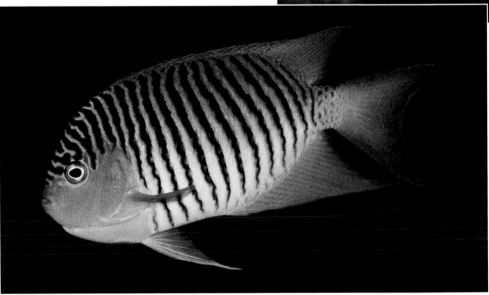

Japanese swallowtail angel
Genicanthus semifasciatus

Less commonly seen in the aquarium trade than some other Genicanthus species, this species has similarities in appearance to G. melanospilos, but the female has a black bar across the base of the tail fin and white and black markings on the operculum, and the male an orange blotch through the head and the front part of the body, none of which are present in G. melanospilos.

WHAT size? *8 in. (20 cm)*
WHAT min size tank? *60 x 24 x 24 in. (150 x 60 x 60 cm)*
WHERE is it from? *Western Pacific Ocean, from southern Japan to northern Philippines.*

Watanabei angel
Genicanthus watanabei

This is a beautiful fish, a subtle, shimmering pale blue in color that looks wonderful under reef aquarium lighting. This is one of the more expensive Genicanthus angels; it is often collected in deep water but will adapt to bright lights.

WHAT size? *6 in. (15 cm)*
WHAT min size tank? *48 x 24 x 24 in. (120 x 60 x 60 cm)*
WHERE is it from? *Wide distribution across the western and central Pacific, from Ryukyu Islands and Taiwan, south to New Caledonia and east to the Austral Islands.*

Lamarck's angel
Genicanthus lamarck

An elegant silver-and-black fish, Lamarck's angel has less obvious differences between males and females than most Genicanthus species. Females (shown above) have a broad black arc running along the lateral line, but this stripe is absent in males.

WHAT size? *10 in. (25 cm)*
WHAT min size tank? *72 x 24 x 24 in. (180 x 60 x 60 cm)*
WHERE is it from? *Indo-Pacific Ocean, Malaysia and Indonesia, from southern Japan to Vanuatu and Great Barrier Reef.*

Pomacanthus imperator

Emperor angel

The emperor angel is one of those fishes that many marine aquarists aspire to keep. It is beautifully colored as an adult and has a very different appearance as a juvenile—the transition between the two is extraordinary. Unfortunately, it is not the easiest of fishes to keep.

WHAT size?
15 in. (38 cm)

WHERE is it from?
Wide range from the Red Sea, across the Indian and Pacific Oceans from East Africa to Hawaii, Line Islands, and Tuamoto Islands, as far north as southern Japan, south to the Austral Islands.

WHERE does it live in the wild?
Juveniles are secretive and live in caves, holes, and under overhangs; adults are found in areas of dense coral growth in lagoons or on reef slopes, often under overhangs or in caves.

WHAT aquarium environment?
Plenty of rockwork with large caves and overhangs but also plenty of swimming space.

WHAT minimum size tank?
72 x 24 x 24 in. (180 x 60 x 60 cm)

WHAT does it eat?
May be difficult to get feeding initially; once established in the aquarium, provide a varied diet, including dried seaweed sheets, algae-based dried food, and frozen crustaceans. Commercial foods formulated for angelfishes are useful. Feed at least three times daily.

HOW hardy?
Large adults often have difficulty adjusting to the aquarium environment and feeding regimen, and may be susceptible to parasitic infections. Juvenile fishes are much better in this respect. Fishes at a size of 3–4 in. (8–10 cm), around the time when they are beginning to change to adult coloration, are probably the best to buy, but even these may have problems.

HOW compatible with other fishes?
Can be aggressive, especially when large, so needs bold, robust companions.

HOW compatible with invertebrates?
Can usually be kept with small-polyp stony corals (*Acropora*

▼ *In time the juvenile pattern fades and the adult pattern emerges.*

▲ *Like many* Pomacanthus *species, as a juvenile the emperor angel has a pattern of swirling blue and white stripes.*

and *Montipora* species, for example) and leather corals and their relatives. Do not keep with fleshy, large-polyp stony corals or tridacnid clams.

WHAT does it cost?
★★☆☆☆   ★★★★★

Cost varies with age and size. Juveniles are reasonably priced; large adults are very expensive.

▼ *The adult emperor angel is a spectacular fish, but not easy to keep in the reef aquarium.*

LARGE ANGELFISHES

The various species of *Pomacanthus, Holacanthus, Chaetodontoplus,* and so on, although stunningly beautiful, have generally been considered to be unsuitable for reef aquariums. Their tendencies to eat or at least damage clams and corals are coupled with, in many cases, large size, a territorial disposition, and difficult husbandry. Some large angels are fairly susceptible to disease; others are difficult to get feeding in the aquarium. However, more recently, some reefkeepers have begun to try keeping these fishes in reef aquarium settings, and with a careful choice of invertebrates have enjoyed some success. The reef aquarium, with its high water quality and abundance of live rock, is a much better environment for these species than the traditional marine fish tank, and makes many of them rather easier to keep. It should be stressed, however, that large angels are fishes for experienced aquarists, and that keeping them in a reef tank is a risky business, as experience is relatively limited.

Pomacanthus navarchus

Majestic angel

The majestic angel lives up to its common name—it is a truly magnificent fish. One of the best larger angels for the reef aquarium, it is not too difficult to keep and is less likely to damage sessile invertebrates than many of its relatives. Like other *Pomacanthus* species, it looks very different as a juvenile, and in this fish the change to adult coloration is rapid—intermediate forms (quite common in some other angels) are seldom seen. It has been reported to eat *Anemonia* "Majano" nuisance anemones.

WHAT size?
11 in. (28 cm)

WHERE is it from?
Indo-Pacific Ocean, from Indonesia to the Philippines, Micronesia, and the Great Barrier Reef, Australia.

WHERE does it live in the wild?
In coral-rich areas in lagoons and protected reef slopes.

WHAT aquarium environment?
Prefers areas of dense rocks and invertebrates, and is bolder when plenty of hiding places are close at hand, but needs plenty of swimming space as well.

WHAT minimum size tank?
72 x 24 x 24 in. (180 x 60 x 60 cm)

WHAT does it eat?
Will adapt to eat most aquarium foods. Seaweed sheets are a good staple, supplemented by a range of frozen crustaceans and flake and pellet foods.

HOW hardy?
A relatively robust species for this family, typically having few problems once established in the aquarium. Large adults, although spectacular, often struggle to adapt to aquarium life, whereas small individuals, in the 3–4 in. (7–10 cm) range, will usually do well if conditions are good. Has been reported to live for over 20 years in the aquarium.

▼ *The majestic angel lives up to its name, and is a better choice for the reef aquarium than most large angels.*

HOW compatible with other fishes?
Often relatively shy initially, especially in juvenile form. Becomes bolder with age, and may be territorial toward similar fishes, but generally ignores unrelated species.

HOW compatible with invertebrates?
Usually safe with small-polyp stony corals, mushroom anemones, leather corals, and their relatives. May eat low-growing soft corals, such as *Xenia* species and star polyps, and risky to keep with fleshy, large-polyp stony corals and tridacnid clams.

WHAT does it cost?
★★★☆☆ ★★★★★

Pomacanthus semicirculatus

Koran angel

PROFILE

A large, bold, hardy species, the Koran angel is so named because of an imagined resemblance to Arabic script of some of the markings on the adult. Juveniles, as in other *Pomacanthus* angels, look very different from the adults. It is not a fish for the average reef aquarium, but can be kept with a limited selection of invertebrates. In this respect, it is typical of many *Pomacanthus* angels.

WHAT size?
16 in. (40 cm)

WHERE is it from?
Red Sea, Indian Ocean, and western Pacific Ocean: from East Africa to New South Wales, Australia; north to southern Japan, south to Lord Howe Island.

WHERE does it live in the wild?
Juveniles live in shallow water in areas protected from strong currents. Adults are found on reefs with dense coral growth that provide plenty of hiding places.

WHAT aquarium environment?
Plenty of cover, providing large caves and overhangs, but also lots of open swimming space.

▶ *Juvenile Koran angels have a pattern characteristic of young* Pomacanthus *species.*

WHAT minimum size tank?
72 x 24 x 24 in. (180 x 60 x 60 cm)

WHAT does it eat?
Dried algae sheets and a wide range of frozen and dried foods. Feed at least twice a day. Will also graze on algae within the aquarium, including cyanobacterial films.

HOW hardy?
Very hardy, particularly for a large angel; juveniles adapt better to aquarium life, but even large adults do better than those of other species.

▼ *This subadult Koran angel still shows traces of the distinctive juvenile pattern.*

HOW compatible with other fishes?
Can be very territorial and aggressive. Needs large, robust tankmates, and should be one of the last fishes added to the tank.

HOW compatible with invertebrates?
Best kept with only the most robust corals, such as leather corals and mushroom anemones.

WHAT does it cost?
★★☆☆☆   ★★★★☆

Pygoplites diacanthus

Regal angel

PROFILE

The regal angel is one of the most dazzling members of a family of beautiful fishes. It is also renowned for being difficult to keep, with a very poor survival rate in traditional marine aquariums. Although this remains a fish for the expert aquarist, this species does much better in reef aquariums, probably because of the grazing opportunities offered by live rock. It is one of the better large angels for the reef aquarium, posing a relatively low risk to corals.

WHAT size?
10 in. (25 cm)

WHERE is it from?
Red Sea, Indian Ocean, and western Pacific: from East Africa to Tuamoto Islands, north to southern Japan, south to Great Barrier Reef and New Caledonia.

WHERE does it live in the wild?
On coral reefs in areas of dense coral growth, often close to caves.

WHAT aquarium environment?
Prefers plenty of cover with lots of caves and crevices.

WHAT minimum size tank? 60 x 24 x 24 in. (150 x 60 x 60 cm)

WHAT does it eat?
Dried algae sheets and flakes and a variety of frozen foods. Often reluctant to accept prepared foods initially; grazing from live rock may help the fish to get past this stage. Feed at least twice daily.

HOW hardy?
Individuals from the Red Sea and Indian Ocean appear to do better than those from the Pacific (the latter have blue-gray coloration on the breast). Can do well in the reef aquarium, but remains a fish for experts. It is best quarantined in a quiet aquarium for several weeks to ensure it is healthy and feeding well before being added to the display aquarium. It is best to buy fishes in the 3–4 in. (7–10 cm) range, as these adapt best to the aquarium.

HOW compatible with other fishes?
Tends to be rather shy and best kept with quiet companions. May be bullied by other angels, the more aggressive tangs, and species such as triggerfishes.

HOW compatible with invertebrates?
Usually leaves most corals alone; very occasionally may damage fleshy, large-polyp stony corals or eat zoanthid polyps.

WHAT does it cost?
★★★★☆ ★★★★★

Centropyge species

Pygmy angels

A few years ago, *Centropyge* angels were routinely recommended as fishes for the reef aquarium. However, experience has shown that many species are far from ideal, as they will eat corals, particularly fleshy, large-polyp stony corals. The situation is further complicated by the fact that although some species are known to be particularly likely to damage corals (the lemonpeel angel, *C. flavissima,* for example), in many others some or even most individuals can be harmless but others will cause problems. Worse, some individual *Centropyge* angels will live in the reef aquarium without problems for long periods, but suddenly become destructive. When keeping *Centropyge* angels in the reef aquarium, you must exercise caution. If in doubt, watch the fish carefully for signs of less-than-angelic behavior.

    Centropyge angels also vary considerably in their hardiness: Some are fairly easy to keep, but many are quite difficult. They feed primarily on algal films and detritus, and sometimes do not easily adapt to prepared foods. In some cases they can live indefinitely without accepting any food offered by the fishkeeper—but only if the aquarium produces enough food. Tanks with living rock provide a great environment for these angels.

WHERE do they live in the wild?
Typically found around reefs or in lagoons, among dense coral growth, usually in small groups that are believed to be haremic, with single males and several females.

WHAT aquarium environment?
Prefer densely packed rocks and invertebrates, which provide both grazing opportunities and cover. Some deep-water species prefer less intense lighting.

WHAT do they eat?
Feed primarily on diatom films and detritus, but most will also eat a variety of dried and frozen foods. The staple diet should be based on algae. Feed at least once daily.

Cherub angel
Centropyge argi ▷

This is one of the smallest Centropyge *angels, and is unusual in that it can become very territorial toward unrelated fishes, especially when it is kept in smaller aquariums. It is generally safe with most corals, but some individuals are exceptions to this. It is usually hardy and easy to keep.*

WHAT size? *3 in. (7 cm)*
WHAT min size tank? *36 x 15 x 12 in. (90 x 38 x 30 cm)*
WHERE is it from? *Western Atlantic Ocean: Gulf of Mexico and the Caribbean Sea from Bermuda and Florida to French Guiana.*

HOW hardy?
Species vary: some easy to keep, others very difficult.

HOW compatible with other fishes?
Should not be kept with others of their own kind, and may be territorial toward other *Centropyge* species. Generally indifferent to unrelated fishes, although there are exceptions.

HOW compatible with invertebrates?
Different species and individuals vary in their safety with corals and clams. In general, best not kept with fleshy, large-polyp stony corals or tridacnid clams.

WHAT do they cost?
★☆☆☆☆   ★★★★★
Most species moderately priced; deep-water fishes such as *C. multicolor* can be very expensive.

African flameback angel
Centropyge acanthops

A very striking species with bright blue and orange coloration, this is similar to the Caribbean flameback angel, C. aurantonotus. *It is a hardy species and usually reasonably safe with invertebrates, but tridacnid clams and fleshy large-polyp stony corals may be at risk.*

WHAT size? 3 in. (8 cm)
WHAT min size tank? 36 x 18 x 15 in. (90 x 45 x 38 cm)
WHERE is it from? Western Indian Ocean, East African coast, Madagascar, Seychelles, Maldives, and other island groups in the area.

Centropyge species

Pygmy angels

△

Coral beauty
Centropyge bispinosa

This is one of the safest Centropyge *angels for the reef tank. It is usually straightforward to keep, as well as living up to its common name. The color on the flanks is highly variable between individuals.*

WHAT size? *4 in. (10 cm)*
WHAT min size tank? *36 x 18 x 15 in. (90 x 45 x 38 cm)*
WHERE is it from? *Wide range across the Indian and Pacific oceans: from East Africa to Tuamoto Islands, north to southern Japan, south to Lord Howe Island.*

Eibl's angel
Centropyge eibli

A beautiful fish with an unusual color scheme, this is one of the easier Centropyge angels to keep. It is best housed with a restricted range of corals, such as leather corals (Sarcophyton species) and their relatives. It is mimicked by juveniles of the Indian Ocean mimic tang, Acanthurus tristis.

WHAT size? *6 in. (15 cm)*
WHAT min size tank? *48 x 18 x 18 in. (120 x 45 x 45 cm)*
WHERE is it from? *Indo-Pacific Ocean, from Sri Lanka to Indonesia and Malaysia.*

White-tail angel
Centropyge flavicaudus

This species has a simple but attractive color scheme and is one of the smallest of the family. It is hardy and generally safe with sessile invertebrates, with the exception of the most vulnerable species.

WHAT size? *3 in. (7.5 cm)*
WHAT min size tank? *36 x 15 x 12 in. (90 x 38 x 30 cm)*
WHERE is it from? *Indo-Pacific Ocean, from East Africa to Tuamoto Islands, southern Japan to New South Wales, Australia.*

Centropyge species

Pygmy angels

Flame angel
Centropyge loricula

This is a dazzling species, but not the easiest of the family to keep. It is quite likely to eat or damage large-polyp stony corals and tridacnid clams, so is best kept with a restricted range of invertebrates.

WHAT size? *6 in. (15 cm)*
WHAT min size tank? *48 x 24 x 18 in. (120 x 60 x 45 cm)*
WHERE is it from? *Wide range across the tropical Pacific Ocean.*

▽

176

Potter's angel
Centropyge potteri

This stunning species is unmistakable. It is quite difficult to keep in traditional marine aquariums, but usually does well in reef tanks with plenty of live rock. It should be kept with only the most resilient of corals, such as leather corals and mushroom anemones. Rare specimens lacking the orange color have been reported.

WHAT size? *4 in. (10 cm)*
WHAT min size tank? *48 x 18 x 15 in. (120 x 45 x 38 cm)*
WHERE is it from? *Hawaii and Johnston Atoll.*

Multicolor angel
Centropyge multicolor

This lovely species is collected in relatively deep water, and prefers less intense lighting. Once acclimatized to the aquarium it usually does well. It can be quite aggressive toward related species. It poses less of a threat to corals and clams than many other Centropyge species, but should still be added to the reef aquarium with caution.

WHAT size? *3.5 in. (9 cm)*
WHAT min size tank? *36 x 18 x 18 in. (90 x 45 x 45 cm)*
WHERE is it from? *Western and central Pacific Ocean: Micronesia, Marshall Islands, Gilbert Islands, Cook Islands, Society Islands, Fiji, and Tonga.*

Centropyge species

Pygmy angels

Keyhole angel
Centropyge tibicen

Growing larger than other
Centropyge *angels, this is a hardy
species with a striking color scheme.
It should be kept only with resilient
invertebrates.*

WHAT size? *7.5 in. (19 cm)*
WHAT min size tank? *60 x 24 x
24 in. (150 x 60 x 60 cm)*
WHERE is it from? *Christmas Island
in the Indian Ocean to Fiji in the
western Pacific, from southern Japan
in the north to Lord Howe Island in
the south.*

Half-black angel
Centropyge vroliki

*A subtly beautiful fish, also known
(appropriately) as the pearlscale
angel, this species sometimes
hybridizes with C. eibli. It is
straightforward to keep, but may
graze on large-polyp corals and
Tridacna species clams. It is
mimicked by juveniles of the mimic
tang, Acanthurus pyroferus.*

WHAT size? *5 in. (12 cm)*
WHAT min size tank? *48 x 18 x
18 in. (120 x 45 x 45 cm)*
WHERE is it from? *Western Pacific
Ocean: Bali to Tonga, southern
Japan to Lord Howe Island; also
around Christmas Island in the
Indian Ocean.*

Butterflyfishes

They may be stunningly beautiful in many cases, but if there is one family of fishes that at face value would seem to be completely unsuitable for the reef aquarium, it would have to be the butterflyfishes (Chaetodontidae). Most butterflyfishes feed on corals, and among them are fishes that cannot be kept in the aquarium because they will eat only living coral polyps, accepting no substitutes. Others, although corals are their primary source of food, will eat other foods, and these butterflyfishes can be kept in fish-only aquariums.

Happily for reef aquarium keepers, a select few butterflyfishes do not feed on corals, and it is among those that the species described here are found. These butterflyfishes include plankton feeders and species that eat small invertebrates from among coral heads. Butterflyfishes in both categories are generally safe with corals and most other sessile invertebrates, although they may eat tubeworms. Also, in some cases caution needs to be exercised with respect to which corals are kept with these species, as fleshy large-polyp stony corals may fall victim, just as they tend to do with other fishes that are on the margins of safety with corals.

Price guide

★	$32–40
★★	$40–48
★★★	$48–56
★★★★	$56–64
★★★★★	$72–96

Copperband butterflyfish

PROFILE

A beautiful silver-and-gold species, with a long, elegant nose, the copperband butterfly is quite popular with reef aquarium enthusiasts because, as well as being attractive and interesting, it can be used to control *Aiptasia* pest anemones. Its effectiveness in *Aiptasia* control is inconsistent—some individuals eat them enthusiastically, whereas others leave them alone. Even if it does not earn its place in the aquarium by eating *Aiptasia*, it remains a beautiful fish, but it is not particularly easy to keep. The closely related margined butterflyfish *(Chelmon marginalis)* is considered to be slightly easier to keep.

WHAT size?
8 in. (20 cm)

WHERE is it from?
Western Pacific, from the Andaman Islands to the Ryukyu Islands and Australia.

WHERE does it live in the wild?
Close to rocky shores and on coral reefs, also found in silty lagoons and estuaries, at depths from 3 to 85 ft. (1–25 m), usually singly or in pairs.

WHAT aquarium environment?
Prefers plenty of live rock to provide both grazing and shelter.

WHAT minimum size tank?
48 x 24 x 24 in. (120 x 60 x 60 cm)

WHAT does it eat?
Once established in the aquarium it will eat most foods, but may sometimes be difficult to get feeding when first introduced to the tank. Feeding frozen mussels, cockles, or clams in their (opened) shells may help, and an aquarium with abundant live rock will provide plenty of more natural grazing opportunities. Feed at least twice daily.

HOW hardy?
May have difficulty adapting to the aquarium (mainly because of feeding issues), but once established is moderately hardy.

HOW compatible with other fishes?
Highly territorial with its own kind, but usually ignores unrelated fishes.

HOW compatible with invertebrates?
Generally safe with most soft corals, small-polyp stony corals and tridacnid clams, as well as shrimps, hermit crabs, starfishes, and snails. Will usually eat *Aiptasia* anemones, tubeworms, and other worms (such as bristleworms), and sometimes will graze on zoanthid polyps and low-growing encrusting soft corals such as star polyps *(Pachyclavularia* species). Will also occasionally nip at fleshy large-polyp stony corals.

WHAT does it cost?
★★★★★

◄ The copperband butterflyfish is stunningly beautiful, but can be difficult to keep in the reef aquarium.

Chaetodon miliaris

Lemon butterflyfish

The lemon butterflyfish is a very attractive species, and very easy to keep by the standards of its family. It feeds primarily on plankton in the wild, which gives it the dual advantage in the reef aquarium of being easy to feed and usually safe with invertebrates. Over time, it is prone to fading of its beautiful yellow color; feeding a good diet may help.

WHAT size?
5 in. (13 cm)

WHERE is it from?
Eastern central Pacific Ocean, Johnston Island, and Hawaii.

WHERE does it live in the wild?
Usually found over shallow reef flats or shallow sea mounts, in schools feeding on plankton, but has been found at depths of up to 825 ft. (250 m).

WHAT aquarium environment?
Prefers plenty of open water and strong currents.

WHAT minimum size tank?
48 x 18 x 18 in. (120 x 45 x 45 cm)

▲ *The lemon butterfly needs a vitamin-rich diet to maintain its lovely pale yellow color.*

WHAT does it eat?
Will eat virtually any frozen or dry foods: frozen crustaceans such as brineshrimp, mysis, and krill, are ideal, as is fish roe. Feeding color-enhancing dry foods and vitamin-enriched products may help to prevent color loss. Feed at least twice daily.

HOW hardy?
Very hardy.

HOW compatible with other fishes?
Peaceful with its own and other species. Can be kept singly, in pairs or groups, but all individuals should be introduced to the aquarium together.

HOW compatible with invertebrates?
Usually safe with all invertebrates; very occasionally may nip at fleshy large-polyp stony corals.

WHAT does it cost?
★★☆☆☆   ★★★★☆

Hemitaurichthys polylepis
Pyramid butterflyfish

PROFILE

This very distinctive orange-and-white species is an excellent reef aquarium butterflyfish. It feeds on plankton, so poses very little threat to sessile invertebrates. The only difficulty in keeping it is the requirement for quite frequent feeds—something it shares with many other planktivorous species.

WHAT size?
7 in. (18 cm)

WHERE is it from?
From Christmas Island in the eastern Indian Ocean, across the Pacific Ocean from Indonesia to the Line Islands, Pitcairn Island, and Hawaii; as far north as southern Japan, south to New Caledonia.

WHERE does it live in the wild?
Found along steep reef walls, in large schools feeding on zooplankton in strong currents, at depths of 10–30 ft. (3–40 m).

WHAT aquarium environment?
Prefers plenty of open swimming space and strong currents.

WHAT minimum size tank?
60 x 24 x 24 in. (150 x 60 x 60 cm)

WHAT does it eat?
Will eat a wide range of frozen and flake foods. Should be fed at least three times per day.

HOW hardy?
Usually a very hardy, robust species.

HOW compatible with other fishes?
Peaceful with other species and can also be kept with its own kind in pairs or groups, provided all individuals are introduced together. May be shy when first introduced to the aquarium, and should be added before any aggressive or boisterous companions.

HOW compatible with invertebrates?
Usually completely safe with invertebrates: has occasionally been reported to nip at *Xenia* and similar corals when very hungry.

WHAT does it cost?
★★☆☆   ★★★☆☆

◀ *The pyramid butterfly is one of the best of its family for the reef aquarium.*

Heniochus diphreutes

Wimplefish

Sometimes known as "the poor man's moorish idol," this striking black, white, and yellow species, with its flamboyant dorsal fin, is one of the best butterflyfishes for the reef aquarium. When buying it, however, be sure not to buy the very similar threadfin bannerfish (*H. acuminatus*), which will eat corals. The two species can be distinguished by differences in their anal fins. In *H. diphreutes*, the rearmost black stripe extends to the tip of the anal fin, whereas in *H. acuminatus* the black stripe does not reach the tip of the fin, which is white.

WHAT size?
8.5 in. (21 cm)

WHERE is it from?
From the Red Sea and East African coast, across the Indian and Pacific Oceans as far as Hawaii.

WHERE does it live in the wild?
Found on outer reef slopes and current-swept channels, often in large schools, feeding on zooplankton. Found at depths ranging from 50 to 660 ft. (15–200 m). Sometimes acts as a cleaner, picking parasites from larger species.

▶ *The wimplefish is an old aquarium favorite and a good choice for the reef tank.*

WHAT aquarium environment?
Needs plenty of swimming space, and prefers strong currents.

WHAT minimum size tank?
60 x 24 x 24 in. (150 x 60 x 60 cm)

WHAT does it eat?
Frozen crustaceans such as mysis, brineshrimp, and krill, and fish roe. Feed at least three times a day.

HOW hardy?
Generally very hardy.

HOW compatible with other fishes?
Generally peaceful with its own and other species; can be kept in pairs or groups. Bold as an adult, but prefers quiet tankmates as a juvenile.

HOW compatible with invertebrates?
Generally harmless to invertebrates; when underfed may occasionally pick at fleshy large-polyp stony corals.

WHAT does it cost?
★★☆☆   ★★★☆☆

Forcipiger species

Longnose butterflyfishes

PROFILE

There are two *Forcipiger* species, both of which can be kept in the reef aquarium. They use their long snouts to reach into crevices in coral heads to feed on small crustaceans, worms, and other creatures. They are both highly attractive species and not too difficult to keep, although the big longnose butterflyfish (*Forcipiger longirostris*) is more of a challenge than the yellow longnose (*F. flavissimus*).

WHERE do they live in the wild?
Found on exposed reefs and in lagoons, at depths from 3 to more than 330 ft. (1–100 m). Usually found singly, in pairs or in small groups.

WHAT aquarium environment?
Prefer plenty of live rock to provide shelter and hunting opportunities.

WHAT do they eat?
Small frozen foods, such as crustaceans and fish roe. The big longnose butterflyfish requires more care in this respect, but a well-established aquarium with plenty of live rock and sand can help by providing a supply of small live foods.

HOW hardy?
Generally hardy provided they are kept well fed.

HOW compatible with other fishes?
Prefer peaceful tankmates, particularly *F. longirostris*, which may have difficulty competing for food with boisterous companions. Should not be kept with their own kind, except in mated pairs.

HOW compatible with invertebrates?
Generally safe with corals but will eat worms, including tubeworms.

WHAT do they cost?
★★☆☆☆   ★★★★☆

Yellow longnose butterflyfish
Forcipiger flavissimus

This lovely species is bolder and easier to keep and feed than F. longirostris, but poses slightly more of a risk to corals and may nip the tube feet off sea urchins and starfishes, a behavior also practiced in the wild.

WHAT size? *9 in. (22 cm)*
WHAT min size tank? *60 x 24 x 24 in. (150 x 60 x 60 cm)*
WHERE is it from? *Very wide range from the Red Sea and East African coast, across the Indian and Pacific Oceans, to Hawaii, Easter Island, the Galapagos, and Baja California; found as far north as southern Japan and as far south as Lord Howe Island.*

Big longnose butterflyfish
Forcipiger longirostris

The very long snout and small mouth of this fascinating species make it rather more difficult to feed than its cousin F. flavissimus. It requires small foods and is best kept with slow-moving, passive fishes to ensure that it gets its fair share.

WHAT size? *9 in. (22 cm)*
WHAT min size tank? *60 x 24 x 24 in. (150 x 60 x 60 cm)*
WHERE is it from? *The Red Sea and East Africa, across the Indian Ocean and western Pacific Ocean to the Marquesas, Hawaii, and Pitcairn Island, north to the Bonin Islands, south to New Caledonia.*

▲ *The yellow longnose butterfly is a good choice for a peaceful reef aquarium, but will eat fanworms.*

Triggerfishes

▶ As a family, the triggerfishes would appear to be among the worst possible fishes for the reef aquarium, given their reputation for eating everything remotely edible, rearranging aquarium décor and damaging equipment, savaging their tankmates, and even removing parts of fishkeepers' fingers. Despite these drawbacks (which many species, unfortunately, do have), triggerfishes are fascinating fishes to keep in the aquarium and have many devotees. They are intelligent fishes that quickly learn to recognize their keepers and respond to them, and in time become real pets.

Fortunately, although many triggerfishes are very destructive in the reef aquarium, a select few can be kept successfully in this setting— with care.

Price guide

★	$40–48
★★	$48–64
★★★	$64–80
★★★★	$80–120
★★★★★	$120–128

Xanthichthys is a small genus of planktivorous triggerfishes. They are found in schools in the wild and tend to be more peaceful with their own species and other fishes than many triggerfishes are. They are hardy fishes, but may be a little shy when first introduced to the aquarium.

WHERE do they live in the wild?
On upper reef slopes and drop-offs, in areas with strong currents, in schools, feeding on zooplankton, at depths ranging from 26 to 300 ft. (8–91 m).

WHAT aquarium environment?
Plenty of open water but some live rock and corals to provide shelter. Strong water movement is preferred.

WHAT do they eat?
Will eat all aquarium foods: Frozen crustaceans and fish roe provide a good substitute for the natural diet. Feed at least twice a day.

HOW hardy?
Generally very hardy.

HOW compatible with other fishes?
Generally peaceful with other robust fishes. Can be kept in pairs or (in extra-large tanks) in small groups.

Xanthichthys **triggerfishes**

HOW compatible with invertebrates?

Safe with corals and clams, but large individuals may eat shrimps.

WHAT do they cost?

★★★☆☆　★★★★★

▼ *Male blue-throat triggers are more colorful than the females. The female lacks the blue color of the male's chin and the gold edges to the fins, but is still an attractive fish (see page 186).*

Blue-throated triggerfish
Xanthichthys auromarginatus

This is the most frequently imported Xanthichthys *species, and probably the best triggerfish for the reef aquarium. Males and females have different coloration—only males have the blue patch on the lower part of the head that gives this species its common name, and the gold edge to the fins that provides the scientific name.*

WHAT size? *12 in. (30 cm)*
WHAT min size tank? *72 x 24 x 24 in. (180 x 60 x 60 cm)*
WHERE is it from? *From the East African coast, across the Indian and Pacific Oceans as far as Hawaii; north to the Ryukyu Islands, south to New Caledonia.*

Crosshatch triggerfish
Xanthichthys mento

A relatively uncommon import, this spectacular fish is very peaceful for a trigger and is usually well behaved in the reef aquarium. This species can be kept in pairs in a large aquarium. Male fishes can be identified by their red tail fin.

WHAT size? *12 in. (30 cm)*
WHAT min size tank? *72 x 24 x 24 in. (180 x 60 x 60 cm)*
WHERE is it from? *Across the Pacific Ocean from southern Japan to southern California, including Marcus Islands, Wake Islands, Hawaii, Pitcairn Island, Easter Island, and the Galapagos.*

Melichthys vidua

Pink-tailed triggerfish

Of the three *Melichthys* species, this is the most frequently seen in the aquarium trade (the others, the Indian triggerfish *M. indica* and the black triggerfish *M. niger*, are also very attractive but grow very large and are not often imported). It is a very peaceful fish, by the standards of triggerfishes, and one of the better species for a suitably large reef aquarium.

WHAT size?
16 in. (40 cm)

▼ *A good triggerfish for a large reef tank, this species is among the more peaceful of the family.*

WHERE is it from?
From East Africa across the Indian and Pacific Oceans to Hawaii, the Marquesas, and Tuamoto, as far north as southern Japan, as far south as New Caledonia.

WHERE does it live in the wild?
Typically found on outer reef slopes, in current-swept, coral-rich areas, at depths of up to 200 ft. (60 m), feeding on zooplankton. Usually seen in small groups.

WHAT aquarium environment?
Prefers strong currents, plenty of open water, and some live rock for cover.

WHAT minimum size tank?
72 x 24 x 24 in. (180 x 60 x 60 cm)

WHAT does it eat?
Will eat all dry and frozen foods. Feed at least twice daily.

HOW hardy?
Very hardy.

HOW compatible with other fishes?
Generally peaceful with unrelated fishes, but large individuals may eat very small tankmates.

HOW compatible with invertebrates?
Harmless to sessile invertebrates, but large individuals may eat shrimps.

WHAT does it cost?
★★☆☆☆

Odonus niger

Niger trigger

PROFILE

The niger trigger is a very beautiful fish—although its red teeth are slightly strange—and it is very common in the aquarium trade and popular with fishkeepers. It is a straightforward fish to keep, but its popularity and availability belie its very large adult size. It may also bite its keeper—take care when working in the tank or if hand-feeding fishes.

WHAT size?
18 in. (45 cm)

WHERE is it from?
From Red Sea and East African coast, across the Indian and western Pacific Oceans to the Marquesas and Society Islands, north to southern Japan, south to New Caledonia.

WHERE does it live in the wild?
In groups on current-swept reef slopes, in coral-rich areas, feeding on zooplankton and sponges, at depths ranging from 17 to 130 ft. (5–40 m).

WHAT aquarium environment?
Needs some shelter, but also plenty of swimming space.

WHAT minimum size tank?
96 x 36 x 36 in. (240 x 90 x 90 cm)

WHAT does it eat?
Will eat all aquarium foods; should be offered a mix of meaty and algae-based foods. Feed at least three times a day.

HOW hardy?
Very hardy.

HOW compatible with other fishes?
Should not be kept with its own kind, but is not usually aggressive toward unrelated species.

HOW compatible with invertebrates?
Will usually ignore corals and clams but may eat sponges from live rock, and large individuals may eat shrimps and small snails.

WHAT does it cost?
★☆☆☆☆   ★★★☆☆

▼ The niger trigger is a beautiful but very large fish, and needs a very large aquarium.

Rabbitfishes

The rabbitfishes are medium-to-large, algae-grazing fishes. They owe their common name to a vague resemblance between the rounded snouts of some species and the faces of rabbits.

Rabbitfishes are related to tangs, and although they share the same dietary preferences, rabbitfishes are generally much hardier, very disease resistant, and tend to be less territorial and aggressive. However, they are not quite as safe with invertebrates. They lack the caudal blades of tangs, but are armed with even more potent defensive weaponry in the form of venomous spines in the dorsal and anal fins. Stings from these are very painful, and although these fishes are not aggressive, take great care when netting them and when working in the aquarium.

Price guide

★	$32–40
★★	$40–56
★★★	$56–64

PROFILE

With the exception of the foxfaces, rabbitfishes have never enjoyed the popularity they deserve in the aquarium. They can be very useful in preventing and dealing with algae problems—they are voracious herbivores, avidly devouring any hair algae or macroalgae in the aquarium.

WHERE do they live in the wild?
They live in coral-rich areas of lagoons and seaward reefs, juveniles typically in schools, adults in pairs or schools. Often found in shallow water, to 16.5 ft. (5 m) deep, although some species are found at depths ranging to 100 ft. (30 m). They feed on seaweed.

WHAT aquarium environment?
Need plenty of swimming space, but also plenty of live rock to provide shelter and grazing opportunities.

WHAT do they eat?
Provide a diet based on algae: dried seaweed sheets and flakes, algae-based pellets, and flake foods. Feed at least twice daily. Will also graze algae growing in the aquarium.

HOW hardy?
Very hardy and disease resistant.

HOW compatible with other fishes?

Reasonably peaceful, except with their own species or closely related fishes. The foxfaces (formerly placed in a separate genus, *Lo*) tend to be more aggressive than the other species. Despite schooling in the wild, most rabbitfishes tend to fight with their own kind in the aquarium, unless a mated pair can be obtained.

HOW compatible with invertebrates?

Will not usually bother corals or clams, but very occasionally will start nipping at corals, most commonly fleshy large-polyp stony corals.

WHAT do they cost?

★☆☆   ★★★

◀ *The Fiji foxface (Siganus uspi) is an occasional import. It requires similar care to other foxfaces.*

Spotted foxface
Siganus unimaculatus

This species and the other foxfaces would probably be more appropriately named "badgerfaces," given their appearance. This is one of the smallest of the family, and more suitable than most for medium-sized aquariums. It is one of the more aggressive rabbitfishes.

WHAT size? *8 in. (20 cm)*
WHAT min size tank? *48 x 18 x 18 in. (120 x 45 x 45 cm)*
WHERE is it from? *Western Pacific Ocean: Ryukyu Islands, the Philippines, and Western Australia.*

▼ *This is one of the most popular rabbitfishes, and easier than most to accommodate in a typical aquarium.*

Rabbitfishes

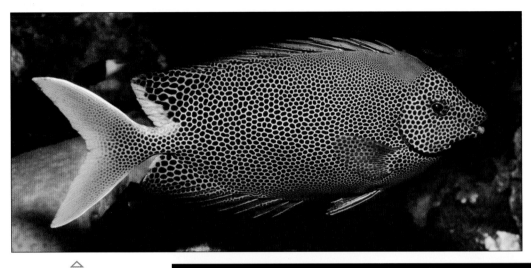

Spotted rabbitfish
Siganus stellatus

This is one of the more commonly imported large rabbitfishes. It is a handsome species but needs a very spacious aquarium. It should be kept well fed to minimize the chances of it eating corals.

WHAT size? *16 in. (40 cm)*
WHAT min size tank? *72 x 24 x 24 in. (180 x 60 x 60 cm)*
WHERE is it from? *Red Sea and Indian Ocean from East Africa to Andaman Islands.*

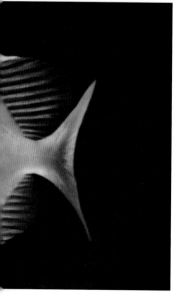

Foxface
Siganus vulpinus

This is probably the most popular rabbitfish with marine fishkeepers, and it is an excellent choice for a large aquarium. It is capable of spectacular color changes; when stressed or sleeping it loses both the yellow body color and the black-and-white stripes on the head, and becomes a mottled light brown with a paler head.

WHAT size? 10 in. (25 cm)
WHAT min size tank? 60 x 24 x 24 in. (150 x 60 x 60 cm)
WHERE is it from? Western Pacific Ocean: the Philippines, Indonesia, New Guinea, Great Barrier Reef, New Caledonia, Vanuatu, Kiribati, Tonga, Caroline Islands, and Marshall Islands.

Barred rabbitfish
Siganus doliatus

This very attractive species is another of the more modestly sized rabbitfishes and makes a very good algae grazer in the aquarium. The two dark bands on the head and the forepart of the body distinguish this species from its relatives.

WHAT size? 10 in. (25 cm)
WHAT min size tank? 60 x 24 x 24 in. (150 x 60 x 60 cm)
WHERE is it from? Western Pacific Ocean, from eastern Indonesia to Tonga, south to northwestern Australia, north to Palau.

Part Three
Aquarium Variations

▶ There are hundreds of different fishes that can be kept in the reef aquarium, but not all of them are suitable for every aquarium, and there are some species that are particularly suited to specific tank setups. In this section, we take a look at some different kinds of reef aquarium to see what types of fishes they suit, and provide a list of appropriate species drawn from those covered in this book. We look at a variety of settings, from peaceful nano-reef communities to aquariums with a selection of invertebrates deliberately restricted to allow a wider range of fishes to be kept; from dimly lit "deep reef" tanks to systems designed for keeping demanding shallow-water corals, with intense illumination and powerful water currents. The selection of fishes for each type of aquarium is based largely on the natural environment of each species, but also on their adaptability to different situations and their compatibility with other fishes.

▶ *Clownfishes in a* Duncanopsammia *coral.*

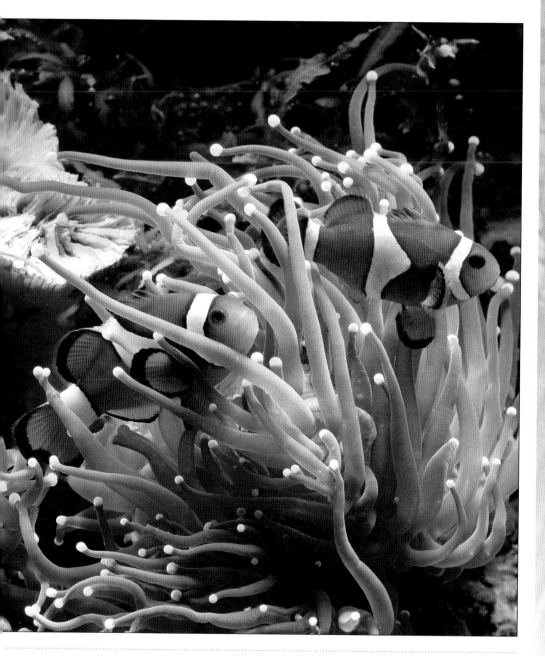

The nano-reef community aquarium

The nano-reef tank is rapidly becoming one of the most popular types of marine aquarium. As the name suggests, nano-reefs are very small, typically ranging from around 12 x 12 x 12 in. to 18 x 18 x 18 in. (30 x 30 x 30 cm to 45 x 45 x 45 cm). Such tanks obviously place stringent restrictions on the size and activity levels of fishes that can be housed in them. When choosing inhabitants for a nano-reef aquarium, be careful to match the size of the fishes to the size of the tank—only the most diminutive fishes are suitable for very small nano-tanks.

When trying to create a community there are still more restrictions. The small living space increases territorial tensions, so extra care is needed in choosing species, as it is essential to do everything possible to avoid combining fishes that might react aggressively to each other. In addition, aquarium conditions may be somewhat unstable, in terms of water quality and temperature, so fishes need to be hardy enough to withstand this.

Single fishes in the nano-reef aquarium

Nano-reef aquariums are ideal for keeping single individuals, or in some cases pairs, of species that are small and hardy, but so territorial or aggressive as to make it difficult to house them with other fishes except in very large tanks. Keeping these species as "pets" like this is very rewarding, as it allows close-up observation of them and avoids the complications of trying to find suitable tankmates.

Below: *Nano-reef community aquariums can house a wide range of attractive small fishes.*

PEACEFUL COMMUNITY FISHES

Chalk bass
(Serranus tortugarum)

Forktails
(Assessor species)

Orchid dottyback
(Pseudochromis fridmani)

Sankey's dottyback
(Pseudochromis sankeyi)

Springer's dottyback
(Pseudochromis springeri)

Painted blenny
(Ecsenius pictus)

Tail-spot blenny
(Ecsenius stigmatura)

Helfrich's firefish
(Nemateleotris helfrichi)

Barber pole goby
(Stonogobiops nematodes)

Clown goby
(Stonogobiops yasha)

Neon gobies
(Elacatinus species)

Coral gobies
(Gobiodon species)

Sand goby
(Fusigobius inframaculatus)

Bluestreak cardinal
(Zoramia leptacanthus)

Left: Many smaller damsels, such as this Chrysiptera taupou, *make good fishes to keep individually in nano-reef aquariums.*

ACTIVE COMMUNITY FISHES

Common clownfish
(Amphiprion ocellaris)

Percula clownfish
(Amphiprion percula)

Orchid dottyback
(Pseudochromis fridmani)

Yellow watchman goby
(Cryptocentrus cinctus)

Pajama wrasse
(Pseudocheilinus hexataenia)

Four-line wrasse
(Pseudocheilinus tetrataenia)

Scarlet hawkfish
(Neocirrhites armatus)

Royal gramma *(Gramma loreto)*

Allen's damsel
(Pomacentrus alleni)

Chalk bass *(Serranus tortugarum)*

Sunrise dottyback
(Pseudochromis flavivertex)

SINGLE FISHES IN THE NANO-REEF AQUARIUM

Common clownfish
(Amphiprion ocellaris)

Percula clownfish
(Amphiprion percula)

Yellowtail blue damsel
(Chrysiptera parasema)

Fiji blue damsel
(Chrysiptera taupou)

Allen's damsel
(Pomacentrus alleni)

Starck's damsel
(Chrysiptera starcki)

Scarlet hawkfish
(Neocirrhites armatus)

Pixie hawkfish
(Cirrhitichthys oxycephalus)

Pajama wrasse
(Pseudocheilinus hexataenia)

Four-line wrasse
(Pseudocheilinus tetrataenia)

Pictichromis dottybacks

Yellow watchman goby
(Cryptocentrus cinctus)
with pistol shrimps

Left: This larger nano-reef aquarium can accommodate a good selection of fishes.

The deep-water reef aquarium

Just about any of the fishes featured in this book will live happily in a deep-water reef aquarium—which is to say a tank with relatively subdued lighting designed around invertebrates that do not need intense illumination. However, there are several species that will actually do much better in this setting than in a more brightly lit system. Most of these species live in deeper water, or in areas with subdued light (in caves or under overhangs) in the wild.

Below: *This tank is stocked with corals that thrive at relatively low light levels, and fishes that come from, or range into, deep water.*

DEEP-WATER REEF FISHES

Genicanthus angels

Longnose hawkfish
(Oxycirrhitus typus)

Flame fairy wrasse
(Cirrhilabrus jordani)

Redmargin fairy wrasse
(Cirrhilabrus rubromarginatus)

Candy hogfish
(Bodianus bimaculatus)

Candycane hogfish
(Bodianus masudai)

Mystery wrasse
(Pseudocheilinus ocellatus)

Squareblock anthias
(Pseudanthias pleurotaenia)

Grammas
(Gramma species)

Tilefishes
(Hoplolatilus species)

Purple firefish
(Nemateleotris decora)

Helfrich's firefish
(Nemateleotris helfrichi)

Lined dartfish
(Ptereleotris grammistes)

Pajama cardinal
(Sphaeramia nematoptera)

Bluestreak cardinal
(Zoramia leptacanthus)

Orange-striped cardinal
(Apogon cyanosoma)

Banggai cardinal
(Pterapogon kauderni)

Yellow cardinal
(Apogon seali)

FISHES FOR THE ROCKY REEF AQUARIUM

Clownfishes (*Amphiprion* species and *Premnas biaculeatus*)

Yellow tang
(*Zebrasoma flavescens*)

Ctenochaetus tangs

Majestic angel
(*Pomacanthus navarchus*)

Regal angel
(*Pygoplites diacanthus*)

Dwarf angels
(*Centropyge* species)

Scarlet hawkfish
(*Neocirrhites armatus*)

Longnose hawkfish
(*Oxycirrhitus typus*)

Red-spotted hawkfish
(*Amblycirrhitus pinos*)

Pixie hawkfish
(*Cirrhitichthys oxycephalus*)

Pseudocheilinus wrasses

Harlequin tuskfish
(*Choerodon fasciatus*)

Fathead, or hawkfish, anthias
(*Serranocirrhitus latus*)

Basses
(*Serranus* species)

Grammas
(*Gramma* species)

Forktails
(*Assessor* species)

Dottybacks
(*Pseudochromis* and
Pictichromis species)

Above: *Rocky reef aquariums such as this provide abundant hiding places, and are ideal for fishes that like plenty of cover.*

Blennies (*Ecsenius*, *Meiacanthus*, *Salarias*, and *Blenniella* species)

Firefishes (*Nemateleotris* species)

Dartfishes (*Ptereleotris* species)

Copperband butterfly
(*Chelmon rostratus*)

Yellow longnose butterfly
(*Forcipiger flavissimus*)

Big longnose butterfly
(*Forcipiger longirostris*)

Neon gobies
(*Elacatinus* species)

Coral gobies (*Gobiodon* species)

Cardinalfishes
(*Apogon*, *Pterapogon*, *Sphaeramia*, and *Zoramia* species)

The rocky reef aquarium

A very popular way of aquascaping reef aquariums involves using a large quantity of live rock and building a slope that rises from close to the front of the tank to high up against the rear glass. Corals are then arranged on top of this slope. This tank layout can look very attractive, but it tends to restrict swimming space and means that the amount of open substrate bed is limited, making the aquarium less suitable for many highly active or sand-dependent species. However, the numerous caves and crevices created by the live rock slope provide a habitat that suits many fishes. Often, these fishes become bolder in the aquarium as a result of the sense of security offered by the extensive cover. The large quantity of rock also provides opportunities for grazing algae and hunting tiny invertebrates.

The sandy aquarium

Sand beds are a key functional part of many modern aquarium systems, but it is possible to create tanks in which the sand bed is the major feature of the setup. By using vertical towers of live rock within the tank and attaching invertebrates to these, and if possible placing most of the live rock required for filtration in a sump, most of the tank base can be given over to an open sand bed. This is particularly suitable for the species listed here. Areas of gravel and rubble are useful for species that like to build burrows.

FISHES FOR THE SANDY AQUARIUM

Halichoeres wrasses

Tilefishes
(*Hoplolatilus* species)

Yellow watchman goby
(*Cryptocentrus cinctus*)

Pinkspotted watchman goby
(*Cryptocentrus leptocephalus*)

Shrimp gobies
(*Stonogobiops* and
Amblyeleotris species)

Above: Yellow watchman gobies with their shrimp companion.

Blue-cheeked goby
(*Valenciennea strigata*)

Orange-spot goby
(*Valenciennea puellaris*)

Ghost goby
(*Valenciennea sexguttata*)

Ornate goby (*Istigobius ornatus*)

Sand goby
(*Fusigobius inframaculatus*)

FISHES FOR THE HIGH-ENERGY ACROPORA AQUARIUM

Clownfishes
(*Amphiprion* species and *Premnas biaculeatus*)

Convict tang *(Acanthurus triostegus)*

Green chromis *(Chromis viridis)*

Yellowtail blue damsel
(Chrysiptera parasema)

Fiji blue damsel *(Chrysiptera taupou)*

Allen's damsel *(Pomacentrus alleni)*

Starck's damsel *(Chrysiptera starcki)*

Powder brown tang
(Acanthurus japonicus)

Powder blue tang
(Acanthurus leucosternon)

Sohal tang
(Acanthurus sohal)

Achilles tang *(Acanthurus achilles)*

Regal tang *(Paracanthurus hepatus)*

Scarlet hawkfish
(Neocirrhites armatus)

Most *Cirrhilabrus* fairy wrasses

Wreckfish
(Pseudanthias squamipinnis)

Bartlett's anthias
(Pseudanthias bartlettorum)

Bicolor anthias
(Pseudanthias bicolor)

Tiger queen anthias
(Pseudanthias lori)

Dottybacks (*Pseudochromis* and *Pictichromis* species)

Midas blenny *(Ecsenius midas)*

Lemon butterfly *(Chaetodon miliaris)*

Pyramid butterfly
(Hemitaurichthys polylepis)

Wimplefish *(Heniochus diphreutes)*

Coral gobies *(Gobiodon* species)

Blue-chin triggerfish
(Xanthichthys auromarginatus)

Crosshatch triggerfish
(Xanthichthys mento)

The high-energy *Acropora* aquarium

Currently enjoying a major vogue are aquariums devoted to *Acropora* and similar small-polyp stony corals. These can be termed high-energy aquariums—and not just because of their electricity consumption. The lighting needs to be intense, and water currents very strong. Water quality is kept very high. Many fishes do well in this type of environment, but those that come from similar environments in the wild will really thrive.

Left: The bright lights and surging currents of an Acropora *aquarium suit most tangs and other fishes found mainly in shallow reef areas.*

The lagoon aquarium

Although small-polyp stony corals such as *Acropora* species are currently fashionable, their demands in terms of intense lighting, very high water quality, and strong water currents lead many reef aquarium keepers to focus on less demanding corals. Popular options are the large-polyp stony corals, such as *Trachyphyllia, Lobophyllia,* and *Scolymia*. In many cases enthusiasts set up aquariums devoted to these types of corals and others that are found in lagoons. These aquariums can be very attractive, but large-polyp stony corals are particularly vulnerable to being eaten or damaged by fishes that might have any tendency at all to nip at sessile invertebrates. Fishes kept with these corals therefore need to be completely safe with corals—borderline species must be excluded.

Below: *Large-polyp stony corals and mushroom anemones dominate this lagoon aquarium— ideal for a wide range of fishes.*

FISHES FOR THE LAGOON AQUARIUM

Clownfishes (*Amphiprion* species and *Premnas biaculeatus*)

Green chromis (*Chromis viridis*)

Yellowtail blue damsel (*Chrysiptera parasema*)

Fiji blue damsel (*Chrysiptera taupou*)

Allen's damsel (*Pomacentrus alleni*)

Starck's damsel (*Chrysiptera starcki*)

Zebrasoma tangs

Ctenochaetus tangs

Genicanthus angelfishes

Fairy wrasses (*Cirrhilabrus* species)

Flasher wrasses (*Paracheilinus* species)

Halichoeres wrasses

Bodianus hogfishes

Scarlet hawkfish (*Neocirrhites armatus*)

Longnose hawkfish (*Oxycirrhitus typus*)

Red-spotted hawkfish (*Amblycirrhitus pinos*)

Pixie hawkfish (*Cirrhitichthys oxycephalus*)

Pseudocheilinus wrasses

Anthias (*Pseudanthias* species)

Fathead, or hawkfish, anthias (*Serranocirrhitus latus*)

Basses (*Serranus* species)

Grammas (*Gramma* species)

Forktails (*Assessor* species)

Dottybacks (*Pseudochromis* and *Pictichromis* species)

Midas blenny (*Ecsenius midas*)

Fang blennies (*Meiacanthus* species)

Firefishes (*Nemateleotris* species)

Dartfishes (*Ptereleotris* species)

Watchman gobies (*Cryptocentrus* species)

Shrimp gobies (*Amblyeleotris* and *Stonogobiops* species)

Neon gobies (*Elacatinus* species)

Coral gobies (*Gobiodon* species)

Cardinalfishes (*Apogon, Pterapogon, Sphaeramia,* and *Zoramia* species)

The robust invertebrate aquarium

Although many of the fishes in this book are completely safe with any invertebrate, there are several species that are a risky proposition to keep with clams and certain corals. Other species may pose a threat to shrimps and small crabs and snails. However, it is possible to create an aquarium that can accommodate both a range of invertebrates and these riskier fishes. The key invertebrates to avoid are tridacnid clams and fleshy large-polyp stony corals. Good choices of sessile invertebrates are mushroom anemones, leather corals and branching soft corals, although for those willing to provide more rigorous aquarium conditions, branching small-polyp stony corals are also unlikely to be bothered by fishes. The popular *Lysmata* shrimps, such as cleaner, fire, and peppermint shrimps, should be avoided when keeping predatory fishes. The large, well-armored boxer shrimp *(Stenopus hispidus)* or one of its relatives is a better bet.

FISHES THAT ARE A THREAT TO SOME CORALS

Emperor angel
(Pomacanthus imperator)

Majestic angel
(Pomacanthus navarchus)

Regal angel *(Pygoplites diacanthus)*

Koran angel
(Pomacanthus semicirculatus)

Centropyge angelfishes

Ecsenius, Blenniella and *Salarias* blennies

Copperband butterfly
(Chelmon rostratus)

Lemon butterfly
(Chaetodon miliaris)

Pyramid butterfly
(Hemitaurichthys polylepis)

Yellow longnose butterfly
(Forcipiger flavissimus)

Big longnose butterfly
(Forcipiger longirostris)

Wimplefish *(Heniochus diphreutes)*

Rabbitfishes *(Siganus* species)

FISHES THAT ARE A THREAT TO SHRIMPS

Pictichromis dottybacks

Longnose hawkfish
(Oxycirrhitus typus)

Red-spotted hawkfish
(Amblycirrhitus pinos)

Pixy hawkfish
(Cirrhitichthys oxycephalus)

Harlequin bass
(Serranus tigrinus)

Tobacco bass
(Serranus tabacarius)

Harlequin tuskfish
(Choerodon fasciatus)

Green wrasse
(Halichoeres chloropterus)

Bluehead wrasse
(Thalassoma bifasciatum)

Rainbow wrasse
(Thalassoma lucasanum)

Torpedo wrasse
(Pseudocoris heteroptera)

Blue-chin triggerfish
(Xanthichthys auromarginatus)

Crosshatch triggerfish
(Xanthichthys mento)

Pink-tailed triggerfish
(Melichthys vidua)

Blue triggerfish
(Odonus niger)

Left: *Small-polyp stony corals are relatively unlikely to be damaged by grazing fishes, so are a good choice for less "reef-safe" species.*

A–Z Common names

A–Z Species names

Credits

The publishers would like to thank the following photographers for providing images, credited here by page number and position: B (Bottom), T (Top), C (Center), BL (Bottom left), etc.

Bioquatic Photo—A.J. Nilsen, NO-4432 Hidrasund, Norway (email: bioquatic@biophoto.net. Website: www. biophoto.net): 22–23(B), 35, 42(T, B), 44, 45(T), 45(BR), 47(T, B), 48, 59, 64–65, 65, 66, 67(T), 69(TL, TR), 77(BR), 78–79, 81(B), 82, 95(T), 109, 110, 113, 120, 121(TL, R), 122, 123(T, B), 125, 129(B), 136(T, B), 137, 140(T, B), 142, 144–145(C), 150(T), 154–155(B), 155(T), 159(B), 161, 162, 164(B), 166(BR), 167, 169(B), 176(T), 177, 187(T), 193(B), 200

Neil Hepworth: 127(T)

Phil Hunt: 53(BR), 72(T), 74, 75(B), 80(T), 93, 94–95, 96, 97, 101(T), 106, 117, 118–119(T), 134(B), 145(T), 146(B), 163(T), 165(TL)

Scott Michael: 49, 55, 58(T), 67(B), 68(B), 71, 76–77(T), 81(T), 84–85(T, B), 85, 90, 91, 98, 107, 130, 131, 134(T), 146(T), 150–151(B), 155(B), 158(T), 174–175(B), 179, 187(B), 188, 192(T),

Geoff Rogers @ Interpet Publishing Ltd: Title page, 2, 2–3(C), 4, 5, 6, 7, 8, 9, 11, 12, 14, 15, 16, 17(TL, BR), 18, 19, 20, 21(T, B), 22(TL), 23(R), 24, 27, 28, 29, 30, 31, 32(BL, TR), 33, 34, 38, 39, 40, 41, 43, 45(C), 50(T, B), 51, 52, 53(CB), 54, 56, 56–57(B), 57, 58(B), 61(T, B), 62–63, 63(T), 68(T), 69(B), 70, 72–73, 73(T, B), 75(T), 76, 79(T), 80(B), 83, 86–87, 87(T, C), 88, 92(L, R), 95(CB), 99, 101(B), 102(T, B), 103, 104–105(B), 105(TL, TR, BR), 108, 111, 112, 114, 115, 116, 119(B), 124, 126, 127(B), 128, 129(T), 132, 133, 135, 138, 139(T, B), 141(TC, BR), 143, 147(TR, CR, BL), 148, 149, 151(T), 152, 153, 154(L), 156, 157, 158(B), 158–159(T), 160, 163(B), 164(T), 165(TR, BR), 166(L), 168, 169(TR), 171, 172–173(B), 173, 174(T), 175(T), 176(BL), 178, 180, 181, 182, 183, 184, 185, 186, 189, 190, 191(T, B), 192(B), 193(T), 195, 196, 197(T, B), 198, 199, 201, 202, 203

Iggy Tavares: 60

Fenton Walsh: 89

Publisher's acknowledgements

The publishers would like to thank the following for their help in providing facilities for photography: Amwell Aquatics, Soham, Cambridgeshire; Cheshire Water Life, Northwich, Cheshire; HB Aquatics, Norwich, Norfolk; Interfish, Wakefield, Yorkshire; Maidenhead Aquatics, Crowland, Lincolnshire; Tuan Pham; Shirley Aquatics, Solihull, Warwickshire; Swallow Aquatics, East Harling, Norfolk; Swallow Aquatics, Gravesend, Kent; Swallow Aquatics, Rayleigh, Essex; Swallow Aquatics, Tenterden, Kent; Wharf Aquatics, Pinxton Nottinghamshire; Tropical Marine Center, Chorleywood, Hertfordshire; World of Fishes, Felbridge, West Sussex.

Publisher's note